I0126782

CONVERSING

WITH

JAMES HILLMAN

City & Soul

JOANNE H. STROUD *(Editor)*
ROBERT SARDELLO *(...)*

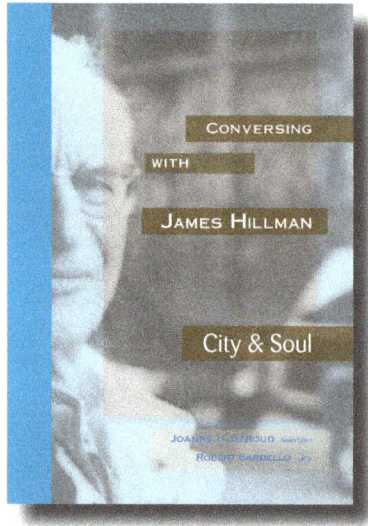

"But first I must thank you for *Conversing with James Hillman: City & Soul*. I've been dipping into it and the content is wonderful (and makes me even more eager to come for the **Alchemical Psychology** event), but what knocked me over was the incredible quality of design and production. I am on a campaign against BAD PRINTING—the drastic decline in legibility in printed books and journals over the past several years—and this book proves that it is not impossible in this day and age to produce a legible, beautiful volume. Congratulations!"

— Jean Hinson Lall

CONVERSING WITH

JAMES HILLMAN

Senex & Puer

CONVERSING WITH

JAMES HILLMAN

Senex & Puer

4TH ANNUAL

THE DALLAS INSTITUTE OF HUMANITIES & CULTURE

JAMES HILLMAN

2015 SYMPOSIUM

JOANNE H. STROUD Series Editor

ROBERT SARDELLO Editor

Conversing with James Hillman

Senex & Puer: James Hillman Symposium 2015

Fourth Annual James Hillman Symposium–*Senex & Puer* was held October 16-17, 2015

The Dallas Institute of Humanities and Culture

Copyright © 2016 Joanne H. Stroud / Dallas Institute Publications

All rights reserved. The Dallas Institute of Humanities and Culture
No part of this book may be used or reproduced in any manner whatsoever without written permission from the publisher except in the case of brief quotations embodied in critical articles and reviews.

Printed in the United States.

Library of Congress Cataloging-in-Publication Data
Stroud, Joanne H.

Conversing with James Hillman Senex & Puer / introduced by Joanne H. Stroud / edited by Robert Sardello

10 digit–ISBN 0-911005-57-9   13 digit–ISBN 978-0-911005-57-8

1. Jungian psychology. 2. Alchemy—Psychological aspects. 3. Jung, C. G. (Carl Gustav), 1875-1961.

Symposium conversing James Hillman's Vol. 3 *SENEX & PUER, Uniform Edition*;
Edited and an introduction by GLEN SLATER, 336 pages, first edition
ISBN: 978-0-88214-581-5

Publications Editors Sarah Theobald-Hall and Laura Gloege
Book design by Suzanna L. Brown, O! Suzanna

Conversing with James Hillman Series

Established in 2014, the *Conversing with James Hillman* series publishes the papers from the James Hillman Symposia, held annually at the **Dallas Institute of Humanities and Culture**. Each symposium takes as its subject a volume of the **Uniform Edition of the Writings of JAMES HILLMAN**. Internationally recognized scholars write papers that explicate the volume and illuminate concepts developed by James Hillman in his ground-breaking work on archetypal psychology. The title of the series, *Conversing with James Hillman*, emphasizes the dialogic nature of this work, considering Hillman's texts in psychological, philosophical, historical, cultural, and social frameworks. Edited by series editor, Joanne Stroud, and volume editor, Robert Sardello, *Conversing with James Hillman* supports the mission of the James Hillman Symposia to honor Hillman's lifelong study of—in his own words, a "psychology deliberately affiliated with the arts, culture, and the history of ideas, arising as they do from the imagination."

The Dallas Institute of Humanities and Culture Publications publishes books that bring disciplines of the imagination—depth psychology, literary criticism, art, architecture, cultural criticism—to focus on the revitalization of culture.

The Dallas Institute of Humanities and Culture
2719 Routh Street, Dallas, Texas 75201 USA 214 871-2440

www.dallasinstitute.org

Table of Contents

PART III: Senex & Puer Revisioning in Art, Poetry, and Culture

PART IV: Extending Arenas of Significance

References

Index

In 1978, James HIllman, above, along with Robert Sardello, Joanne Stroud, Gail Thomas, Donald Cowan and Louise Cowan, co-founded The Dallas Institute of Humanities and Culture in Dallas, Texas.

About James Hillman

JAMES HILLMAN (b. 1926 – d. 2011) was a pioneering psychologist whose imaginative psychology has entered cultural history, affecting lives and minds in a wide range of fields. He is considered the originator of Archetypal Psychology. Hillman received his Ph.D. from the University of Zurich in 1959 where he studied with Carl Jung and held the first directorship at the C. G. Jung Institute until 1969. In 1970, he became the editor of **SPRING JOURNAL**, a publication dedicated to psychology, philosophy, mythology, arts, humanities, and cultural issues and to the advancement of Archetypal Psychology. Hillman returned to the United States to take the job of Dean of Graduate Studies at the University of Dallas after the first International Archetypal Conference was held there. Hillman, in 1978 along with Gail Thomas, Joanne Stroud, Robert Sardello, Louise Cowan, and Donald Cowan, co-founded The Dallas Institute of Humanities and Culture in Dallas, Texas. *The Uniform Edition of The Writings of James Hillman* is published by Spring Publications, Inc. in conjunction with The Dallas Institute of Humanities and Culture.

The body of his work comprises scholarly studies in several fields including psychology, philosophy, mythology, art, and cultural studies. For the creativity of his thinking, the author of *A Terrible Love of War* (2004), *The Force of Character and the Lasting Life* (1999), and *Soul's Code: In Search of Character and Calling* (1996) was on the *New York Times* best-seller list for nearly a year. *Re-Visioning Psychology* (1975), which was nominated for a Pulitzer Prize, *The Myth of Analysis* (1972), and *Suicide and the Soul* (1964) received many honors, including the Medal of the Presidency of the Italian Republic. He held distinguished lectureships at the Universities of Yale, Princeton, Chicago, and Syracuse, and his books have been translated into some twenty languages.

The influences shaping the core of Hillman's work are not limited to depth psychology. His ideas have firm grounding in the classical Greek tradition and are also deeply influenced by Renaissance thought and Romanticism, encompassing the contributions of psychologists, philosophers, poets, and alchemists. Hillman described his own line of thought as part of the lineage of Heraclitus, Plato, Plotinus, Vico, Ficino, Schelling, Coleridge, Dilthey, Freud, and Jung. Other influential authors in Hillman´s work are Keats, Bachelard, Corbin, Nietzsche, Paracelsus, and Shelley.

Throughout his writings, Hillman criticized the literal, materialistic, and reductive perspectives that often dominate the psychological and cultural arenas. He insisted on giving psyche its rightful place in psychology and culture, fundamentally through imagination, metaphor, art, and myth. That act he called soul-making, a term borrowed from Keats.

He is recognized as one of the most important radical critics and innovators of contemporary culture.

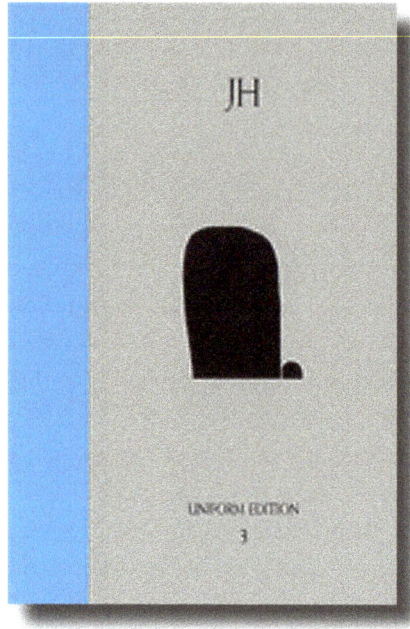

SENEX & PUER

Uniform Edition Vol. 3   JAMES HILLMAN

Edited and Introduction by **GLEN SLATER**

This volume, for the first time, collects James Hillman's running encounters with a primary psychological pattern, an archetype that arises alongside the very attempt to fashion psychological perspective. *Senex* and *puer* are Latin terms for "old man" and "youth," and personify the poles of tradition, stasis, structure, and authority on one side, and immediacy, wandering, invention and idealism on the other. The senex consolidates, grounds and disciplines; the puer flashes with insight and thrives on fantasy and creativity. These diverging, conflicting tendencies are ultimately interdependent, forming two faces of the one configuration, each face never far from the other. "Old" and "new" may be the most direct terms for the pair.

Spring Publications, in conjunction with The Dallas Institute of Humanities and Culture, publishes the *Uniform Edition of the Writings of JAMES HILLMAN*, the founder of ARCHETYPAL PSYCHOLOGY—the lasting legacy of an original mind.

The Uniform Edition, a clothbound set of 11 volumes of the writings of James Hillman (also available as ebooks), unites major lectures, occasional writings, scholarly essays, clinical papers, and interviews arranged thematically. Each volume is embossed with a drawing by the American artist James Lee Byars.

ROBERT SARDELLO

Preface

ARCHETYPAL PUER AND SENEX, youth-ing and aging, the imaginal soul-governors of the very ways soul manifests as life in the world, might easily by called the archetype of all archetypes. It is a kind of meta-archetypal action, to follow the insightful lead of Glen Slater. The papers in this volume inherently express this overarching quality, as the range of topics is incredibly varied, and yet an immediately perceived coherence and resonance can be felt among the contributors.

It might be helpful in this preface to bring out something of the resonance itself, as that can be a kind of guide through the array of creativeness that you are about to enter.

The Array

Resolutions to the split between archetypal senex and puer found in: Homer, physics, harmony, jazz, the spiraling soul's return/elevation/spirit connection, poetry, the city. Explorations of either senex or puer in film, and as governing the dizzying decline of thinking due to computers. Extending the imagination of the archetypal pair in the horizontal direction, and as world gestures, and as meta-archetype, and as the necessary ending and thus ever-beginning of archetypal psychology, and, as well, the way through static understanding into generative, active world unfolding.

The Cohering Resonance

What makes this particular archetypal imagination so compelling, so all-encompassing? What was Hillman seeing, ever more clearly through the years, all the while this imaginal presence kept hiding itself, revealing only a small bit at a time, and only with great and concerted effort? An effort, first, of the continual noticing, out of the corner of the eye, the prevalence of this presence, as if it comes close to reaching a boundary, and on the other side of the boundary can be found completeness, but never quite being able to cross over.

James Hillman found his destiny within the puer-senex archetypal imagination. It follows him through the whole of his life, compelling him to confront it and re-confront it in myriad ways. Thus, more than any other of his interests, this individual, intimate presence allows him gradually to enter into it deeply, with more acuity, attentiveness, and tending than perhaps any of his other work, as important and ground-breaking as it is.

The ability to investigate who you are takes archetypal psychology out of being a theory, while at the same time avoids the terrible pitfalls of any personalism. Thus, following Hillman's trail through "his" archetypal pattern of life serves as the most important model for anyone engaged in archetypal psychology. Anyone seriously interested and engaged in the work of archetypal psychology remains only an intellectual innovator, or a commentator, unless this level of engagement is found.

Destiny is another word for Life. I do not mean living, that daily bearing of joys and difficulties, holding up, moving on, being stuck, sailing along, moments of happiness, many moments of unhappiness, desires and hopes, working, contributing; this is all "living." Life is something different. It is the container of living; it is the being here. Not many of us are, in this sense, here. We are where our thoughts are at any moment, or where our fantasies are, or our hopes and desires, or we are with what we have been, thinking as having to do with the past, using that past to think with, and thus thinking that is past, or we are caught by emotion of one sort or another, and not here. Or we are within memory somewhere. We cannot find our destiny because we are not "here." We are living but are not in contact with Life.

In many ways, depth psychology has made its way into the world by its interest in not being "here." Hillman breaks, one could even say, utterly shatters, the very bread and butter of depth psychology through his exploring of his impersonal destiny, the archetypal dimension of time, not outer time, and really, not inner time, but the time sense of being here.

Life, of course, is always here, whether we are with it in awareness or not. The still prevailing split, explored in many of these papers, are really pathologies of absence. We are pulled somewhere into the not-yet, the could-be, or should-be, the looking and the longing, and with it, the intense and compelling dangers of being out there. Or we are within the has-been, of the past, of memory, of intellectualizing, of holding on to what is known, closed in, walled in, hardening. But *senex-et-puer,* what Hillman calls sameness, is here.

The pathologies can be of help in getting here. That is the importance of going into them individually, as, for example, in the ways explored by Sarah Jackson in film. Seen through this archetype of time, though, the sufferings of not-being-here are effective only when/if they move us to the redemption of life. Perhaps the most important cultural manifestation of not-being-here is given in Scott Becker's revelation of the archetypal action of computer living. The correction becomes possible when we, as does Becker, see through the phenomenon without judging what may be happening in the world through not-being-here. Describing it, yes; but the moment judgment enters, beware, for there is the indication that an archetypal exploration has become mentalized, and is not an exploration of one's impersonal destiny, for when it is such an exploration in depth of one's own being, it is simultaneously for the sake of the world. It is a fine line, discernable in all of these papers. We can decry what is going on within culture as a suffering participant, while at the same time, seeing the corrective inherent in becoming aware, not of, but *within* the pathology.

Marks of Being Here

Senex-et-puer, being-here, does not consist of presence to the linear moment. When we are here, time becomes spacious. We are always here, with. The essays in this volume resonate this sensibility. For example, the oath-taking in the *Odyssey* described by Dennis Slattery is a primary mode of being-with. The same importance can be seen in Gustavo Barcellos' work on the sibling archetype, for we can truly be with our brother, our sister, in ways that generational presence does not break through. Or we can be here when we are fully aware within nature and the world, as so beautifully pictured by Gail Thomas. Or, we can be here, probably in the most intense way possible, through language, poetic language, as described by Joanne Stroud. Or we can get to being-here, by incorporating our own destruction within what we build with our mind and even our heart, as so poignantly spoken by Gustavo Beck, and indeed as James Hillman erases himself at the end of *Re-visioning Psychology*, in an attempt to assure that a senex system of Archetypal Psychology is not established, that it does not become an institution taught in institutional ways.

The living marks of being-here really have to do with entering into Life, which is going beyond by holding in conscious tension whatever may have hold of us, whatever may be forming our personality or personalities from moment to moment, going beyond anticipations and desires, and being able to notice the "container" of archetypal patterns. The container is the now. We are always within the now. Now is happening all the time. It is not duration, nor is it cosmic, nor is it linear, for each now that is now, is new, and dying simultaneously. It is the Janus moment, the *senex-et-puer* moment; it is Hillman's "sameness," which is always happening.

How do we know that we are here, or at least when we are here? Many clues are revealed in these papers.

Language. Language is primary. Mostly, words are no longer connected with presences. Misuse, over-use, going outside of context, repetition; all these contribute to the ineffectiveness of language in being-here. Take the word 'love.' This word has become trivialized. A television ad recently featured the words, "I love my laxative." Or, in another ad, the person on the phone receiving instructions on what to pick up the grocery store says, "Ok, I'll get the dishwasher cleaner. I love you, bye." Archetypal psychology, indeed depth psychology, holds a few words as something more than functional, informational, instructional, and nominalist—words that have to do with being: love, death, God, eternity, void,

I, true. These types of words need to remain sparse, for they are realities of the now, the spacious now that has not manifested as objects. These words are not artificial words; they are "container of the now" words. Adulterate such words, and the now turns into a silly moment between before and next. No one of the papers in this volume trivializes language, and thus the mere reading of them is therapeutic, a way of being with present archetypal presences, who visit in the space between the puer-senex, but only when they are being held, by awareness, in tension. In the "between," we find truly objective words, words that are eternity here.

Character. Depth and archetypal psychology have more than proven that we are whoever is forming the psyche at the moment. We are many masks, many personalities. When masks are worn without awareness, we are somewhere behind them, but have identified with the masks and cannot take them off—and are not here. They may perhaps loosen a bit through depth therapies, and one can even become welcoming of archetypal presences when we are imaginally awake. Something else happens, however, when being-in-time awareness awakes through holding the tension of *senex-et-puer*. Personalities begin to dissolve, and character shows. Individuality is the way it is spoken of in depth psychology, but going the route of the now changes this. For this to happen, the primary ways of not-being-here—thinking and emotional reaction—must diminish. Not through mystical awareness, or years of meditation practice, but by noticing when and how the puer identities and the senex identities pull one way and the other, and noticing, then living, the sameness. Gradually. In this volume, Cheryl Sanders-Sardello, Tom Cheetham, and Randolph Severson orient us toward this true north. I am happy that so many of the presenters of the James Hillman Symposia, here, are such characters!

World. We know when we are here, or when we are not self-consciously here. When the world, with nature most central, and we are one. This latter, nature-and-us as one is the model for being-here. All of nature is exactly what it is, individual and whole, and every aspect in union with every other aspect, fully here. Nothing of nature tries to be something else, except perhaps viruses. When world, in the sense of nature, and we are one, the experience has come to be called "synchronicity." This term is somewhat unfortunate, as the word obscures the fact that being-here, wholly, is being within this kind of simultaneous time, and this time is fully and completely natural; it is the way we are meant to live, fully, naturally, worldly. Clock time, believing in and existing as if clock time were real time gives rise to the puer-senex split—or is it that the split gives rise to linear time? Dividing time when it is simultaneity rather than linearity, separates us from this world and, as well, archetypal awareness.

James Hillman's ultimate work, concern with the Soul of the World, which he entered in earnest here in Dallas (because Dallas is where, strangely, it was happening) was never just an add-on interest, one that many of his colleagues in Jungian psychology did not and still cannot fathom. It is, ultimately, his destiny to which he remained true, no matter where it would take him. If one is true to the *senex-et-puer* tension, one lands right in the middle of earth as imaginal presence, nature as the spiritual-earth. World is slightly different. World is to nature as personality is to character. And, as personalities, world is in need of archetypal therapy. Hillman saw this. Hillman's ultimate interest, we could say, concerned world character.

No-thing. Rodney Teague's paper beautifully ushers us into the ultimate background of the manner in which archetypal psychology concerns activity rather than content, of imaginal as no-thing, and thus being here as yielding to the erasing and creating that is the infinite moment of now. Hillman is so incredibly creative because he was able to notice without categories, without interfering intellectualizing—though he lived within the living idea. He was, pretty much all the time, where he was. If it was within emotion, he became emotion. If it was within idea, he became idea. He could, in a flash, become any moment. It was his gift, but it was also hard-won and tracked, tracked as the many writings of the third volume of the *Uniform Edition*. This tracking is invaluable, as it is the only available guide on living, now, here, in the world, with nature, with others, archetypally. Perhaps this present volume is truest to James's destiny and does not divert from it.

XVIII

Part I:

Reminisces

Robert Sardello, Cheryl Sanders-Sardello

JOANNE H. STROUD

Introduction

FIRST, AND OF SINGULAR importance, I want to dedicate this volume to one of the dearest people I have ever known—CHERYL SANDERS-SARDELLO. Cheryl made one of her last public appearances participating in the 16-17 October 2015 James Hillman Symposium. Very soon afterward, she was struck down with a pulmonary thrombosis. She lay in a coma for two weeks before leaving this world peacefully with the accompaniment of Terese Cullen's ecstatic harp music. Perhaps we might speculate that Cheryl had some intuition about leaving this world at an early age. Much of her life work and teaching was concerned with ways to understand the meaning of death-in-life and life-in-death. For all of her accomplished but truncated life, Cheryl added sweetness and consideration to each occasion. Even those participants in the James Hillman Symposia who had only known her for a short time were touched by her presence and felt keenly our mutual loss.

It is a challenge to introduce properly the subject of the 2015 James Hillman Symposium—Senex & Puer but knowing some Latin might help. In its simplest meaning, just as *senex* means "old," which relates to "senior" or "senator," *puer* means "young." Our word "puerile" derives from it. But what have these so very different phases of human life have to do with one another? It turns out that the answer is: everything.

It is typical of Hillman to turn everything around and upside down, speaking about senex and puer rather than the more usual Jungian way of puer, first, followed by senex. Jung defined the puer-senex relationship as a compelling archetypal complex, with the two extremes tethered together. Jung coined the phrase, which roughly stands for more than just the physiological traits of young age and old age. Each of these characteristics are aspect of personality that are invaluable—the spirited, flashing brilliance of the *puer eternus* mode along with the stability of the senex. I associate an archetype, any of them, with the image of a see-saw, continually shifting back and forth through each day, ever dynamic, tilting one way or the other throughout the whole journey of life from its beginning to its end. When a newborn baby first thrusts out its hand and says "no" or "mine," it is establishing borders and manifesting its early senex side.

Hillman raised this complex to a singular level of significance, placing even more emphasis on its reverberations than Jung did. The James Hillman Symposium of 2015, by focusing on multiple aspects of the puer-senex complex, made all of us more aware of the source of much of the division in our twenty-first century world. The problem, in evidence in the catastrophic inability to tolerate differences or to even address them with any openness today, is in actuality the splitting of seemingly opposite polarities—conservatives versus liberals in political life, showing up as well in the uncompromising rigidity of fundamentalism versus modernism in religious realms. Black is black and white is white, with no softening grey in-between. On one hand, we experience too many absolute, rigid boundaries that constrain in modes of behavior or dress (mufhtis covering the entire body of women) versus unbounded freedom from all restrictions (public nudity and selfies of sexual parts of the body). For better comprehension of the dynamics in our individual relationships, and for better possibility of plumbing the pressing issues of our time, we can benefit by learning how to understand each one-sided extreme. Actually, in my opinion, this may be James Hillman's finest work. It is vital for coping with the strain of fractured polarities that puzzle us. As you learn more about the operation of this complex, you may be surprised at how it manifests in your life. When I dream of flying off on a glamorous trip, or some wild adventure, I recognize that my Peter Pan puer side, like the Sirens call, is luring me. When I suddenly get the urge to bring order to my kitchen shelf by alphabetizing the spices, (very helpful by the way), I know that my latent senex just checked in.

We had a distinguished group of experts from many parts of the world addressing these critical issues and engaging in presentations and dialogue. We began by watching a film that was edited by Judy Kelly from Hillman's three-day conference on the puer-senex complex at Pacifica in 2010, bringing James's sparkling presence into the symposium. For those people in our Dallas audience who never knew James while he was alive, the film showed not only his amazing intelligence but also his urbane wit and throw-away humor.

Then, after many reunions, we assembled in the parking lot behind the back of the Dallas Institute's main building. We were challenged to turn a bleak area, which we call the Bamboo Garden, as it is surrounded by bamboo, into an attractive space for an outdoor barbecue dinner. From the photographs by Kim McBride, Sarah Theobald-Hall, and Suzanna Brown, I think you can see that it actually worked. After dinner, Margot McLean put us in an imaginative mood by reading poetry and engaging in a brief question-and-answer period, with the audience eager to hear about the personal side of James's life. This presentation was followed by Nor Hall's tribute to Hillman, reading and reflecting on Japanese death haiku, the condensed poetry that Jim so enjoyed. This page from Nor's memoir, inspired by her research, was exhibited at a show of Margot's works at Pacifica for their *Climates of Change* conference. A copy is included here so look especially carefully down at the right-hand corner (fig. 1).

Generally I keep dreambook & day-journas together (for 50 years) but separate from WORK notes. Last night's dream came strongly clouded with dirt from the Underworld — graying the white horse and dusting the old coat of the old man. There was a series of steps up from the earth-packed basement store room leaving me unsure as to how to get the horse out. Another woman — an ARTIST full of compassion is down there...She will do it by touch of her hand. Wanting to be here, this dream registers 1) the dust of the beyond, the Bardo, the basement archives where disintegrating paper makes us sneeze. "Dust will be my food." — Egyptian Book of the Dead — 2)And the role of the hand that facilitates Transition between below and above.

IIΛ IIIΧ II

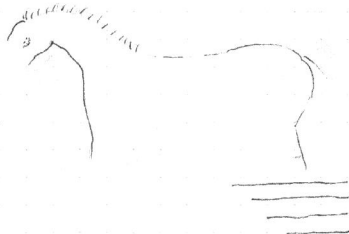

G fig 24

ref. Magdalenian Cave, Bernifal & Font-de-Gaume
15,000 – 13,000 BCE

seed
The stone is alive in my hand,
crops will be thick in my death year.
— Ezra Pound

After Ellen Kennedy (Michels)
drawing Fig 4. IN THE MOON & THE VIRGIN

HQ
1206
.H235
1980

Curious as a reader in libraries to pull my own book off the shelf — had never registered its call # — and see the markings. Poignant — Superstarring from Hell: p34!

HELL for Olson, is being "imageless."

How shall he who is not happy, who has been made so unclear, who is no longer privileged to be at ease, who, in this brush, stands reluctant, imageless, unpleasured, caught in a sort of hell, how shall he convert this underbrush, how turn this unbidden place how trace and arch again the necessary goddess?
— In Cold Hell, In Thicket

✱ MANY WOMEN UNDERTAKE THIS MODERN FORM OF RITUAL WITHDRAWAL INTO THE UNKNOWN SELF BECAUSE THEY FEEL THEY ARE NOT BEAUTIFUL ... THE WORLD AT LARGE, NOT JUST WOMAN, IS "CAUGHT IN A SORT OF HELL," ESTRANGED ... ✱

It bears repeating. How) stands he who is not happy imageless

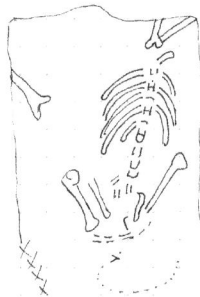

excerpt from Gimbutas CIVILIZATION OF GODDESS p374 fig 10-19
c. 3000 BCE

Thoughts on Kinds of Books bones of the book — Hillman note
Box 107
apparently 1960's - 70's hard to tell because of how notes on scraps of paper are bundled and issue of PROVENANCE and ORIGINAL ORDER according to archive knowledge. Did someone sweep the papers up thus?

Day 8.
Publisher Q

JH asks (typewritten) top of single page:

Could one do a book that was only a group of SKELETAL BOOKS? ala Borges...

Not the whole worked out, but the skeletons...

for example the one on the poetic basis of mind
for example the one on Joyce is the symptom
for example the puer in very abbreviated form.

Figure 1. Nor Hall, Day Page 7. OPUS Archives, Pacifica Graduate Institute.

Lastly, Richard Lewis demonstrated the ingenious way that he works in New York City's public schools to draw young children into connecting with the essence of their creativity. By just holding up the fingers to catch the air, the imagination of children (and of adults, too, just try it) begins to flow. In response, Matthew Green read from the pages of Antoine de Saint-Exupéry's *The Little Prince* that have meant much to him as a teaching device. Larry Allums engaged them in a discussion on imagination and took questions from the audience. We cherish our interactive sessions with the audience.

Saturday morning started with a convivial continental breakfast. We then reassembled to begin in earnest the discussions of this particular volume. All of the presenters, many of whom had been here in previous years, had agreed beforehand to talk, not read their papers. I was grateful for the unanimous response, everyone entering into this mode wholeheartedly, knowing that for us academic types, even though we know the material well, that it sometimes feels risky to ad lib. This approach seemed more faithful to the slightly risky puer spirit of James, than to the comfortable, sensible senex one. Three close friends and allies, Gail Thomas, Dennis Slattery, and Randy Severson, could not be with us in person but wrote papers that are vital, so we have interspersed them throughout in the appropriate sections of the book. It may make for some awkwardness to suture together the actual order of the symposium presentations with the three themes, which were not established at the onset but were suggested later when we read them more closely. As always, our goal is to carry forward the distinctions between recycled Jung wisdom and Hillman's original thoughts.

Pat Berry and I had the pleasure, as session leaders, of introducing the first session, which now in this volume is called The Theoretical Importance of Senex & Puer in Archetypal Psychology: Foundation and Extensions. Pat Berry said, borrowing a line from Glen Slater's Introduction to volume 3: "James Hillman undoes . . . It's about moments of inspiration. He is senex and puer . . . his daimon worked with those two forces. His genius is about both of those things. That's why he's not a man of system, a man of models. It's a revisioning where he lays down the basis of these things."

Before I knew him in person I had admired Glen from reading his profound Introduction to Hillman's *Senex & Puer.* In his paper, "Hillman's Metapsychology," Glen does an extraordinarily good job of relating the theme of puer-senex to many of Hillman's other works. He says that we shouldn't try to follow Hillman; we should try to follow the daimon that animated him. In Glen's delineation of puer tendencies and necessities, I was particularly struck by this statement about the spirit and everyday realities: "The puer, the spirit, the peak needs the anima, the soul, the vale" (p. 39). Glen aptly circumscribes our work, Hillman's friends and followers, in pointing out, "The very term 'archetypal imagination,' . . . is a union of sames, uniting the immediate and particular with the timeless and the universal" (p. 38). That clue was an eye-opening observation, reinforcing the vitality of the work. It sounds easy, but we know that it isn't. Glen recalls Hillman's assertion of the centrality of the puer-senex archetype: "*[T]his specific archetype will be involved with the process character of any complex*" (p. 37). Since so many issues of conflict involve complexes, this assertion reminds the audience of the tenacious grip of all archetypal complexes; complexes need to individuate and reveal their "daimonic aspect and full archetypal significance" through the union of sames (p. 37). Often, what we think of as opposites turn out to have overlapping sameness.

Rodney Teague thinks that part of what Hillman is doing involves trying to help us to imagine better. Rodney brilliantly describes how "Archetypal Thinking as Imaginal Practice" is foundational. He introduces the wisdom of the *Tao-te-ching*, "as it elucidates the harmonious interplay of seeming opposites and the folly of false polarity." Rodney summarizes fully the difficulty of drawing together the split in the senex-puer archetype in this paragraph:

> Rapprochement "in order to heal a fundamental split" between senex and puer–what Hillman describes as the "main work of psychoanalysis" (p. 39)—requires harmonization of senex-puer sensibilities. One works toward harmony through increasing awareness of the operations and activities of senex-puer and by practicing the way of ambivalence, holding the tension of paradox. This is the work of cultivating imaginal ego. We wrestle with the impossibility of easy categorization into boxes labeled "youth" and "old age," "innovation," or "stagnation." Confronted with the questions of technology, we can ignore neither the tantalizing moist spark of creative eruptions nor the world-effacing monolith of "big data." Like the senex-puer archetype as described in its ambivalent wholeness, imaginal ego is discontinuous, uroboric; "a circulation of the light *and* the darkness" (1960, p. 184). As we contend with archetypal paradox, we gain familiarity with "psychic reality," understood as the imaginal world, with an ultimate aim of more faithfully imagining the real (p. 185). (pp. 44-45)

Tom Cheetham in "Errands to an Adjoining Zone" writes about Hillman's connection, or sometimes lack of connection, with Henry Corbin. Tom explains: "The central pillar of Corbin's psychocosmology is the act of spiritual transformation known in Arabic as *ta'wil. Ta'wil* is spiritual hermeneutics, and is, he says, 'the mainspring of every spirituality.' *Ta'wil* is the interpretation of a text or of the world read as a text, which acts as an alchemical elixir for the human soul" (p. 49). I do like the idea of *Ta'wil*. This statement dovetails nicely with our subject matter for the 2016 Hillman Symposium, *Alchemical Psychology*. Tom takes James to task for writing psychology poetically, saying that they can't be done together. Here, Tom quotes Robert Duncan with a rather pointed criticism, in which I do not concur, of Hillman's style. It is a long quotation but worth examining in some detail:

> In a lecture delivered in Buffalo in 1983 for the Analytical Psychology Society of Western New York the poet Robert Duncan (1996) talked about Hillman's work. He said Hillman wanted it both ways. He wanted a poetic psychology. But Duncan warned that it isn't possible. Poetry and science don't mix. He said that Hillman talks as if he were doing psychology, but he never produces any evidence! I think Duncan is a bit harsh and that Hillman often managed to straddle the divide, but he was absolutely right that there is some critical difference between the imagination as it operates in art and poetry, in the wilds of the psyche so to speak, and as it operates at the meta-level of archetypal psychology.

Tom continues to quote Duncan: "Duncan felt this most forcefully in Hillman's alchemical writings. In these Duncan thought he very nearly breaks into poetry" (p. 51). I must say that I can't agree. Though it isn't often accomplished, Gaston Bachelard, the renowned French philosopher of science, does indeed advance the notion that the observations of science and rhythms and images of poetry do inform each other.

Cheryl Sanders-Sardello's essay, "You Have the Right to Remain Silent," from the 2014 Hillman Symposium on City and Soul (which you can find in the first *Conversing with James Hillman* volume) now seems eerily predictive. Soon after the following year's symposium, held in October 2015, she was destined to be utterly silenced. The subject seems preparatory, so intuitive of what befell her. The "Big" in Cheryl's title for this volume "On Being Too Big: Senex-Puer Contemplations" refers to the magnitude of encompassing the senex-puer archetype, which Hillman argues is so foundational, so dominant, so large: "This archetype, these archetypes that spread out around us from this collection; they are so, well, big that they 'back' all psychology; they are a foundation for ego. The puer-senex archetype raises the human being out of the simple dualism of body/spirit (that declaration in Constantinople and Nicea)" (p. 55). Cheryl nails the issue of the conflict in discussions of the soul/spirit split with the following quote:

Puer-senex is the keystone to the bodily knowing self as spirit-soul expression and spiritual reality of being embedded in matter. Our different psychologies have masked the possibility of balance by being either all about the past or all about the future. Whether officially split by the church, or situationally split by life, the split becomes the genesis of pathology, and the place ego becomes trapped. In an ideal world senex-puer would be balanced, in harmony, in rhythm. Perhaps all psychologies would be based on finding balanced tension, maybe they all are. Nevertheless, the split seems somewhat ingrained, and it encourages radical expressions—even soul-less expressions—of one-sidedness. Most recently expressed by exalting in narcissism, encouraging a vacuous adherence to baseless opinions as if they were absolute truths. Where we once looked to our pathologies to find where the gods manifested for modern humanity, we now anesthetize ourselves with mindless newsertainment and assert our interpretational-opinionization rather than seek the truth about anything. (Perhaps one could blame technology.) (pp. 55-56)

Finally, Cheryl sums up the dilemma currently facing us of resolving the conflicting opposites with the required action of forgiveness that is only possible in one's heart on the soul level:

The past requires forgiveness, and, for the puer, the past requires justice. Forgiveness seems most likely in the puer universe, but is hard to understand, as it is located in the soul as a realm one enters, not an act one does. The will does not forgive. The ego does not forgive. The soul forgives through entering the place of the heart where forgiveness is a way of being, not an act to be done. Forgiveness is the very realm in which soul comes to wholeness within one's being in the world, being embodied as individual. Forgiveness expands the soul, becomes the place of the balanced human being. (p. 56)

Why is forgiveness so hard in the glaring reminders of harsh memories or agonizing situations when it is can be so efficacious?

The second session on Saturday morning included Gustavo Barcellos and myself with Robert Sardello and Scott Churchill as session leaders. We have added Gail Thomas's and Dennis Slattery's papers under the grouping of Senex & Puer Revisioning in Art, Poetry, and Culture. In my essay, "Poetry Weaves Together the Split in the Senex-Puer Archetype," I addressed the original way that Hillman focuses on splicing together the split of the senex-puer archetype.

My contention is that great poetry, which often ties together incompatible oppo-sites, can provide a paradigm to bridge the split in the senex and puer archetype. Hillman (2005) enlarges the conception of the equally adamant nature of both puer and senex: "As the senex is perfected through time, the puer is primordi-ally perfect. Therefore there is no development; development means devolution, a loss and fall and restriction of possibilities" (p. 52). So, for all its characteristic changeability and flightiness, the puer, like the senex, at its core resists develop-ment. Hillman points a finger at the ego and consciousness itself as the originat-ing source of splitting and division, therefore approaching warring oppositions through ego development is doomed from the start. Hillman charges us, his readers, his followers, with the heavy duty of seeking union through therapy on the archetype itself. Therefore: *Our attempt at rapprochement shall go by way of returning to the original condition of the archetype before it has been bro-ken apart and turned against itself"* (p. 39; emphasis in original). Hillman does not shy from using the word *soul* as the essential factor for making amalgamations of stringent oppositions:

> The soul itself stands amidst all sorts of opposites as 'the third factor.' . . . [T]he soul holds polarities in harmony . . . But now, the ego, having replaced the soul as the center of conscious person-ality, cannot hold the tension. With its destructive rationalism it makes divisions where the soul gives feeling connections and mythic unities. So the soul has come unstrung; its suffering and illness reflect the torn condition of the split archetype. (p. 40)

I sincerely believe and attempted to demonstrate that a surprising pathway to the healing that only soul and heart can further exists through poetry. I could have chosen many other poems to back up my assertion, but I picked one by my favorite poet, William Butler Yeats, "The Song of Wandering Aengus," to demon-strate this prescription.

Gail Thomas's delightful, imaginary conversation with James, while strolling in Thompson, Connecticut, captures the whole theme of our endeavor: that of *conversing,* or carrying on and pondering over James's words. Gail directs a question to James: "Why is the title of this volume *Senex & Puer* and not the other way around?" which I'm certain that the rest of us have wondered as well. Certainly, James never favored the conventional. He always wanted to shake things up starting from the first page. Then she wonders why he titled the third chapter "'Notes on Opportunism,' not on 'Opportunity,'" a word often used to describe the city of Dallas. This marvelous duet between Gail and James brings in the soaring image of Pegasus and his inspirational, imaginal hoof that sparks creativity when it strikes the ground. Pegasus is the Dallas Institute's founding mascot, in fact the image graces the plaza, and the flying, red horse is dear to

Dallasites since it once topped the Magnolia Building as the city's highest sky-scraper. Gail also speaks of John Neely Bryan and the mythic stories of the founding myth of the city, from the beginning, seizing the "*kairotic* moment–an opening, a possibility, available at a very special moment in time" (p. 69). Does it sound pretentious if I say that Dallasites seem inclined to grasp the jolt of the moment for "offering opportunity and new beginnings" (p. 69)? We have to confess, as citizens of Dallas, much puer spirit governs us. Certainly, James belonged here for part of his journey—with that inspirational genius we treasure.

Gustavo Barcellos's essay, "Notes on Horizontality: Continuity, Penetration, Soul, and the Sibling Archetype," takes the reader into the relationship of the puer archetype with ascentionality. This vertical mode, often characterized by "ambition, competition, arrogance and what psychology now calls 'inflation'" (p. 71) is contrasted with the horizontal world of soul. Gustavo quotes Hillman (2005) as indicating that the very nature of *puer* consciousness is to ignore "the daily world and its 'incessant continuity'" (p. 159), which is the world that Gustavo admires, the horizontal world of brotherhood. Gustavo suggests that this "incessant continuity" of our daily world "would lead us away from the *puer,* in order to get us closer to soul, leading us from verticality to horizontality: an anti-heroic move" (p.71). Gustavo finds in the brother archetype a welcome contrast to the asymmetry of parental relationships. These, even when loving, "will always hide the specter of power and domination" (p. 74). It is only the "sibling impact," as he calls it (he infers the sibling sister as well), "that translates more precisely into the experience of real assimilation and appreciation of *diversity*" (p. 74). Gustavo echoes something of Hillman's thought in the chapter "Peaks and Vales." The spirit moves upward (and the *puer eternus* is a spirit phenomenon), but the vale is the is the place of soul-making (thank you, Keats).

Dennis Slattery addresses the chapter "Puer Wounds and Odysseus' Scar" from volume 3 in his provocative paper. He brings together Odysseus' famous identifying scar with his oath-taking as remembrance of the original wound. Dennis jogs our memory to an important clue, sometimes forgotten, of the necessity of wounding as characteristic of the puer complex. In this paragraph Dennis reminds us,

> crippling is indispensable for this figure. He achieves a greater viability through his vulnerability (p. 223). Senex qualities, on the other hand, include "judgment, sobriety, prudence, deviousness, isolation, and suffering" yet he has "little power" (p. 238). Odysseus, Hillman argues, is a combination of senex-puer energies, attitudes and dispositions. Running parallel with the Greek hero is a series of oaths that run like a red thread through the epic, beginning in Book Two and ending the epic in Book Twenty-Four. The oath itself is best grasped as a senex-puer creation holding energies of

both figures in a tension that allows for peace to be maintained if the terms of the oath are honored by the conflicting energies of seemingly irreconcilable forces. Under the oath rubric I also include pacts, truces, cease-fires as well of other forms of mutually agreed-upon compromises that allows the tension of opposites and oppositions to sustain a harmony through a written code or set of agreed-upon conditions. Here resides one of the contemporary values of Hillman's astonishing insights into the wound (pp. 214-44). (pp.78-81)

Dennis provides an amalgam, or weaving together, of senex and puer qualities in a convincing example from Homer's *Odyssey.*

Sarah Jackson's "Puer Women and Female Heroes in Film" laments that Hillman concentrated on the masculine aspects of the puer without giving enough credence to the feminine puer spirit. In relating to chapter 4 of *Senex & Puer*, "The Great Mother, Her Son, Her Hero, and the Puer," she chooses examples in film to demonstrate her premise that females as well as males can also be guided by the puer. Those who attended the conference had the advantage of seeing the film stills Sarah presented with her talk. Glen Slater remarked that Hillman had resistance to the idea of hope. Sarah said most films today with female puer figures are not very hopeful. I remember heated talk with James about the idea of "Progress," which he believed should always be tempered.

Over boxed lunches we separated into four breakout groups to discuss the film that we viewed the evening before of Hillman discussing the puer and senex at Pacifica. I wish to thank here Scott Churchill, Robert Leaver, Bob Kuglemann, Klaus Ottmann, Larry Allums, Gustavo Barcellos, and Judy and Pat Kelly for their work in directing the discussions. The groups were heralded by many participants as leading, literally, to major breakouts in their ideas of the book and Hillman's work on these archetypes.

We began the afternoon with Pat Berry and Glen Slater as leaders for session III. This session seemed to get heavily into the senex mode; this grouping comes under Extending Arenas of Significance in this volume.

Robert Sardello never fails to deepen any awareness of the soul's role in the world, and he ran true to form in his essay, "The Rhythmical Character of Hillman's *Senex-et-Puer.*" He points out that Hillman's emphasis differs from Jung's in a most significant way: "James Hillman's extensive efforts to 'see through' what was known in Jung's psychology as two archetypes—that of the senex and of the puer—into his brilliant and scintillating *senex-et-puer* perspective may well be his most important contribution to the creation of Archetypal Psychology" (p. 101). Sardello also captures the playful yet serious nature of much of Hillman's writings: "He provides ways to resolve the polarities of the archetypal image by developing the concept of 'sameness,' seeing the one within the other—always—

thus coming to be able to 'play seriously' and 'seriously play'" (p. 101). I need to also urge you to read, if you haven't already, Robert's compelling preface to this volume, which does such a fine job of summing up the work to be done in fathoming the depths of this archetype.

In this time of raucous literalizations, Sardello calls for residing within the heart center, not relying exclusively on the thinking mode as our culture inclines toward. He dialogues with the current overriding view of theoretical physics that the earth's history began with the Big Bang, arguing that this image invades our culture, pushing us always toward explosion. This pervasive image of "infinite destructiveness" and apocalyptic expectation blocks access to the wisdom of the heart, knowledge carried to the heart. Explaining why this work has such ramification, Sardello arrived at this conclusion: "We are unable to see the rhythms of creation past containing the future and the future containing the past, both persisting simultaneously because the archetypal complex of a senex-puer split governs us. Living within the 'spacious presence' requires heart-awareness, our 'middle realm,' and earth is also the 'heart' of the cosmos. Were we able to surrender to senex-et-puer we would see everything as rhythms in symphonic harmony" (p. 104).

Scott Becker always brings our discussions into the present moment, the *zeitgeist*. His "Titanomachy: Finding Senex & Puer in the Twenty-first Century" caused a stir. The audience asked many questions, trying to respond to the alarming thought that technology for all the obvious ways it seeks to connect and make community actually delivers separation and alienation. We are "increasingly overwhelmed by the digitized, accelerated, and increasingly chaotic world of technological overload. . . . We are losing our minds, but we don't seem to mind," Scott warns (p. 107). In other words, "[The] symptoms of our time are anesthesia, apathy, and amnesia, and together they constitute a powerful threat to our capacity to learn from the past, engage the present, and imagine our future" (p. 107). Scott follows this frightful prediction with questioning about what myths are we currently living, which is difficult "when our capacity to engage in mythic understanding is itself fading." Scott suggests that Hillman, not unusually, can be our guide, pointing out that Hillman, in his essay "...And Huge is Ugly: Zeus and the Titans," defined Titanism as "an inflated, monstrous world created by the absence of the Olympian gods" (p. 107). In exploring the impact of the Titanic world, we can find the symptoms outlined above: "anesthesia, apathy, and amnesia."

Scott further defines the symptom of anesthesia, as "psychic numbing" (Robert Lifton's term) or "doubling" (Robert Sardello's term) in which we are not fully present, not in touch with either conscience in our minds or with animal instincts in our bodies. Scott details this serious flaw so characteristic of our blighted culture: "In a very concrete, measurable sense, we are losing our depth and our capacity to remember, to care, to focus, and to imagine. The positive forms of senex and puer consciousness are being eroded from within, our peaks and vales flattened by our flat screens. So the first symptom of our time is anesthesia, in both the literal and the metaphorical sense: the incapacity to synthesize, to breathe in the beauty and pain of the world, to imagine" (p. 109). Without revealing any more of Scott's invaluable insights into our cultural moment, I urge you to read his paper in its entirety. Glen Slater added that we have made a religion of technology.

Gustavo Beck brings the melancholy of mourning into focus in his paper, "The Hidden Senex and the Dying Puer: A Eulogy to James Hillman's Monotheistic Polytheism." His point of view that Hillman's puer side is now dying and turning into senex rot is challenging to say the least. If this premise were literally true, it could seem like a repudiation of all our efforts in recollecting Hillman's texts. That seems exactly what we wish to avoid: turning James's vital works into some ossified article to simply sit in a library bookshelf. I, for one, enjoy tying into Hillman's puer side.

In a joyful contretemps, Randy Severson speaks of Hillman as "the jazz poet," which taps into Hillman's writing with its brilliant puer virtuosity style:

> Hillman was a great poet because Hillman was a jazz poet. I don't know if Hillman got jazz, but jazz got him. Think of his prose, think of his writing. Albert Murray or Stanley Crouch would be his best interpreter. I'm neither one of these, but I do love jazz. Hillman's writing—if that's what we are going to call it—is almost pure jazz in style: it is extraordinarily, frustratingly complex; it's marked by intricate, strong propulsive rhythms; it's improvisational, characterized by those extraordinary riffs, virtuosic solos; its free, wide-ranging and yet there's always something essentially Hillman about it, some essential melodic line. (pp. 123-124)

Randy explains further that jazz, like James, ultimately is both puer and senex, soul and spirit:

> Hillman's texts do converse with one another. Jazz is conversation—"a nuanced, swift and complicated one," as Wynton Marsalis says. . . .
>
> Music is spirit. Language is soul. Music that is language, that is conversation, is jazz, spirit finding soul, the union of puer and psyche. Language that is musical, language that is jazz: melodious, metered, democratic, conversational is soul-finding spirit, psyche-finding puer. And like jazz at its best and at its worst, Hillman perseverates; he goes on and on. Hillman is always saying the same thing, but he never says it the same way twice, and if it's not said the same way, it's not the same thing. (p. 124)

It is my opinion that Hillman, who tap-danced and sang (a duet, "You Don't Need Analyzing," once with Margot McLean at Duquesne), and also wrote and spoke in such creative ways, would have cherished being called a jazz poet.

In summary, I think Hillman's directive to his friends and followers remains valid: *"Therefore our concern must be with archetypal therapy or therapy of the archetype"* (2005, p. 36; my emphasis). I take this charge seriously: whenever and wherever, to see through separations and recognize the bridges that connect any seeming opposites in individual personality or situations one to the other. Glen Slater so clearly expresses the call: "We still live in a time in which the polarization of this archetypal configuration dominates. . . . In the Information Age, with its adoption of technological-solutionism, the new has all but abandoned the old, and across the globe the old is staging a desperate, destructive, regressive retribution in all forms of fundamentalism. . . . In hearing once again this base note of Hillman's thought, perhaps we might see where and how we might still be makeweights" (p. 40).

We ended the day by returning to the highs of the puer mood by watching a video that Margot McLean brought of James tap dancing with a group of high school girls in a gym. Then we gathered for wine and food and drumming on the porch, which has become a tradition—Suzanna Brown keeping pace with the Brazilian contingent. Almost everyone was moved to join in either drumming or dancing on a warm, beautiful evening.

I have written this Introduction to provide readers who were not here in Dallas with the feeling of actually being at the symposium. Now that we have heard and read the papers, we have rearranged them for inner coherence in this volume. In culling kernels from the above essays, I am guilty of choosing what jumped out to me. You, the reader, will need to read them to see if you agree. After all, this endeavor is an ongoing conversation, isn't it?

Margot McLean is a visual artist who lives and works in New York City and rural Connecticut. She has collaborated with James Hillman on many projects, including *Permeability*, for the Art & Psyche Conference, San Francisco, CA; *Shadows of the Earth*, Schumacher College, Totnes, UK; *The Human Place in the Natural World*, Nathan Cummings Foundation, New York, NY; and *Dream Animals* (1997, Chronicle Books). Her work has been exhibited internationally (Italy, Ireland, Japan): including *catching light, migrations, water flow, extinctions*, La Specola Natural History Museum, Florence; and *Plant, Animal, Habitat*, The Cathedral of St. John the Divine, New York, NY.

MARGOT MCLEAN

Senex & Puer: An Oblique Approach

After one has abandoned a belief in God,
poetry is that essence which takes its place as life's redemption.
　　　　　　　　　　　　　—Wallace Stevens (1957)

Don't bear me ill will, speech, that I borrow weighty words,
then labor heavily so that they may seem light.
　　　　　　　　　　　　　—Wislawa Szymborska (1996)

JAMES HILLMAN LOVED poetry. He loved the poet's way, the poet's language. He loved reading poems out loud. He loved flipping through a book of poems hoping to land on a surprise or to find an old friend. Although he only wrote poems for himself, his writing became more and more poetic as the years passed; lightening the language while retaining its depth.

For this reason, I felt it appropriate to read poems that related to the subject of senex and puer at the Dallas Institute gathering. I wanted to approach the subject obliquely and through the lens of art. (The titles of the poems I read are listed here.)

James also remained firmly engaged in the political world throughout his life. As we are approaching the election of 2016, I'd like to quote a passage from the first chapter of the *Uniform Edition,* volume 3, *Senex & Puer,* which was written over ten years ago, in 2005:

> The division is in the political world with its aging leaders and systems attempting to maintain "law and order," and the rebellions of youth in the name of "rights and freedom." As one legal philosopher has put it: never in the history of the United States have we had so many laws, so much science of law and its enforcement, and never have we had so much disorder and violence. (p. 32)

And then James characteristically turns to poetry to clarify his point by quoting William Butler Yeats:

> The falcon cannot hear the falconer;
> Things fall apart; the centre cannot hold;
> Mere anarchy is loosed upon the world,
> The blood-dimmed tide is loosed. . .
> The best lack all conviction, while the worst
> Are full of passionate intensity. (p. 32)

Poems read on Friday evening at the James Hillman Symposium 2015:

"You Reading This, Be Ready," by William Stafford

"You and Art," by William Stafford

"Growing Up," by William Stafford

"Henry Manley, Living Alone, Keeps Time," by Maxine Kumin

"Monet Refuses The Operation," by Lisel Mueller

"'Passing Through'—*on my seventy-ninth birthday*," by Stanley Kunitz

"Shapes," by Ruth Stone

"Those Winter Sundays," Robert Hayden

"Tired Sex," by Chana Bloch

"The Resemblance Between Your Life And A Dog," by Robert Bly

"on the way down," by Ko Un

"A Disappointment," by Louis Jenkins

"Across the Swamp," by Olav H. Hauge (trans. by Robert Bly)

"Walking on Tiptoe," Ted Kooser

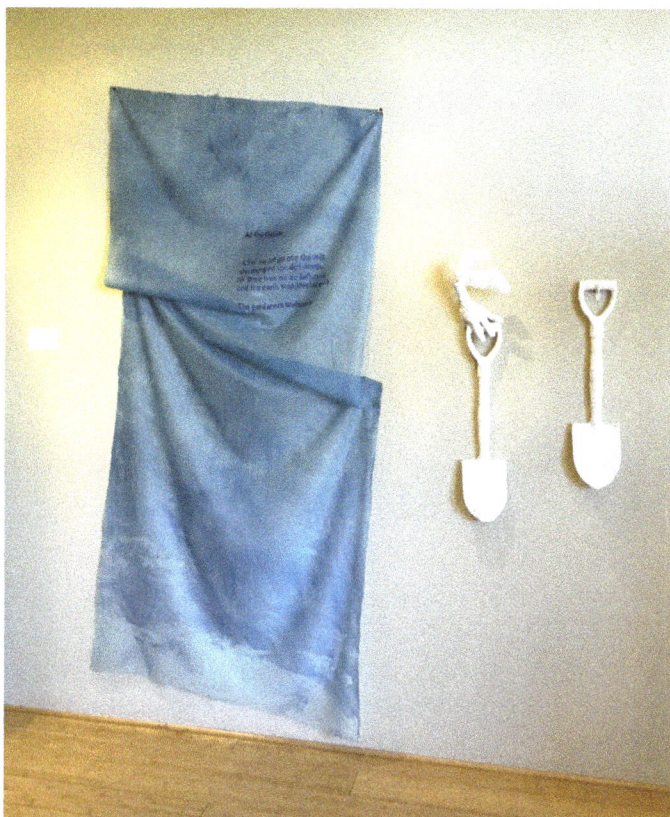

Margot McLean
At the Grave, 2016
in response to Mermer Blakeslee's poem
42" x 72" fabric, acrylic, pencil
as shown at Pacifica Graduate Institute.
Detail below

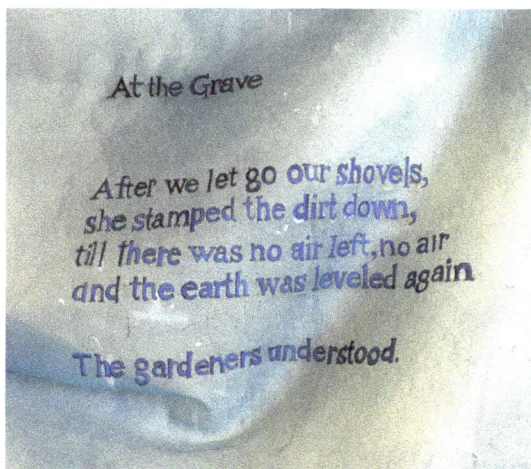

At the Grave

After we let go our shovels,
she stamped the dirt down,
till there was no air left, no air
and the earth was leveled again

The gardeners understood.

Nor Hall is a writer, theatre artist, and psychotherapist. Author of the chapbook *Traces* and books including *Irons in the Fire, Those Women*, and *The Moon and the Virgin*, Hall writes on a variety of topics inspired by art and artists. She has presented at the Eranos Institute on gender, at the Minneapolis College of Art and Design on Lou Andreas-Salome, and on the Architecture of Intimacy at the Dallas Institute. Dramaturg for the award-winning Archipelago Company in Chapel Hill since 1996, Hall currently enjoys collaborating on performance research projects in the Twin Cities and is an advisor for Pantheatre's Myth and Theatre festival in France. She volunteers at the Center for Victims of Torture, co-chairs the Walker Art Center's Producers Council, and is distracted by thirteen grandchildren.

Conversing in Memoriam

THINKING OF JAMES Hillman "becoming an ancestor," as he says in *The Force of Character* (1999), and leaving the making sense of a life to us. He left an un-published note, wondering about a new form of book: "Could one do a book that was only a group of skeletal books?" (OPUS Archives, Hillman Collection, [Box 107], Pacifica Graduate Institute). This impersonal question of his and others more per-sonal ("Is dreaming still important to you?") inform my work on an archetypal graphic memoir. Day Page 7 from working in the OPUS Archives in the Spring of 2015 ends on the bottom right hand corner (becoming Day 8) in a recorso with the skeletal reflections of the senex returning his thoughts to the puer (fig. 1). The fragment of Persephone from my memoir Page 2 (fig. 2) refers obliquely to Mar-got McLean's Pacifica exhibition "Handling It" in which these pages are shown, and the following Day Page 6 (fig. 3), which draws on the Hillman Collection (Box 196 A, Jungiana), addresses our frequent conversations on the value of the image which I now continue in writing and drawing by hand.

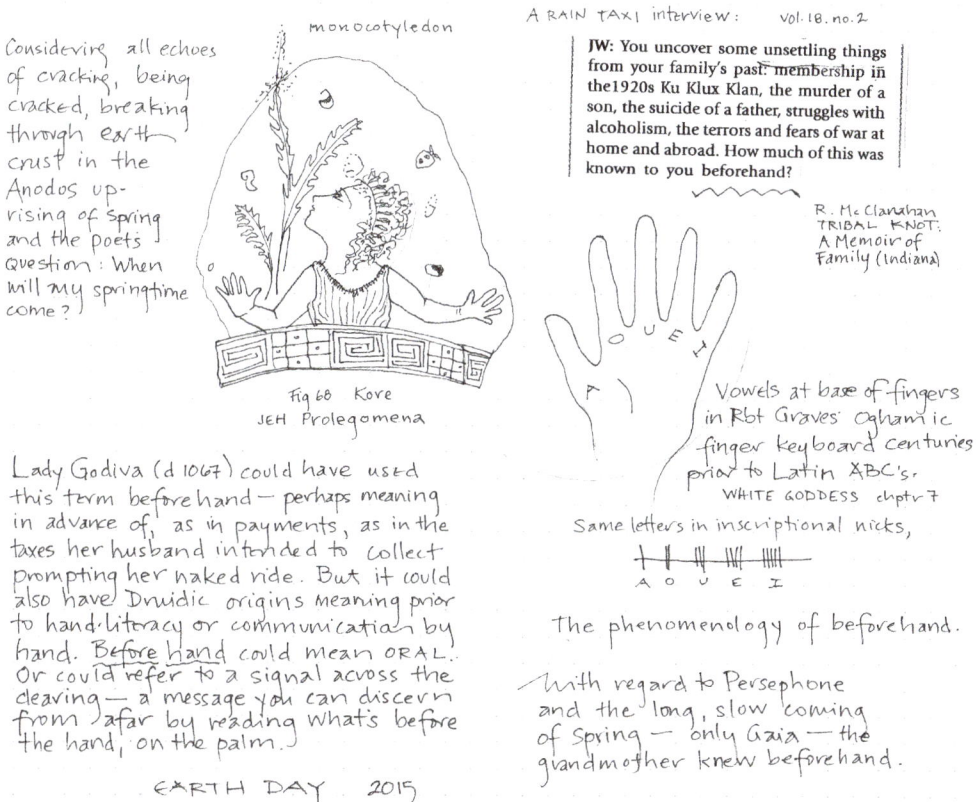

monocotyledon

Considering all echoes of cracking, being cracked, breaking through earth crust in the Anodos up-rising of spring and the poet's Question: When will my springtime come?

Fig 68 Kore
JEH Prolegomena

Lady Godiva (d 1067) could have used this term beforehand — perhaps meaning in advance of, as in payments, as in the taxes her husband intended to collect prompting her naked ride. But it could also have Druidic origins meaning prior to hand-literacy or communication by hand. Before hand could mean ORAL. Or could refer to a signal across the clearing — a message you can discern from afar by reading what's before the hand, on the palm.

EARTH DAY 2015

A RAIN TAXI interview: vol. 18. no. 2

JW: You uncover some unsettling things from your family's past: membership in the 1920s Ku Klux Klan, the murder of a son, the suicide of a father, struggles with alcoholism, the terrors and fears of war at home and abroad. How much of this was known to you beforehand?

R. McClanahan
TRIBAL KNOT:
A Memoir of
Family (Indiana)

Vowels at base of fingers in Rbt Graves' Oghamic finger keyboard centuries prior to Latin ABC's.
WHITE GODDESS chptr 7
Same letters in inscriptional nicks,

A O U E I

the phenomenology of beforehand.

With regard to Persephone and the long, slow coming of spring — only Gaia — the grandmother knew beforehand.

Figure 2

Senex & Puer: The James Hillman Symposium 2015

Praise to the BOOK CARRIERS who work in the stacks!
Safron Rossi who curates, Jennifer Maxon who archives, &
Richard Buchen who guards Special Collections and told
the story of Marija Gimbutas escaping the Soviets to run
from Kaunas, Lithuania with a baby under one arm
and her dissertation under the other. (8 July 1944)

WAR STORIES   MG's family were book carriers
risking deportation by smuggling
Lithuanian books into the country.
She would write 28 books & over 300
articles on European pre-history. pp10-11

THE CIRCLE IS UNBROKEN : A BRIEF BIOGRAPHY
— Joan Marler, From the Realm of the Ancestors

(Box 116)

(19 June 1942) L-804
. Joseph Campbell to Ed Ricketts.
  —almost finished a large reading project on mythology
  "which has been scratching at my brain"... "Jean will
  be dancing at Bennington"... "What I want to do
  is get through with all my long-time projects before
  returning to New York for what may be the
  damndest winter of the twentieth century."

Hillman Box 196A*
JH notes toward publishing
  "Driving Miss Edith" whose
  chauffeur took a break from
  the Swiss Army to work for
  her for 7 years — driving
  Mrs. E. Rockefeller McCormick &
  family to analytical sessions
  with Jung. She hypnotized
  her driver by hyper-neuroses
  who followed her to Chicago
  to sue. Great writing.

Emile Ammann
Im Dienste der reichsten Frau
Leben und Abenteuer
eines Chauffeurs,
Montana. Verlag A.G. 1933?

* JUNGIANA

DID YOU SEE HER
DRESS?! IT'S NEO-
LITHIC DESIGN!!
AND CHECK OUT HER
SIGNAL ARMS.

LEGENDARY COUTURE
  snake
  water
  breast

Day 6.   6.5 hrs

Hungarian
6th c. BCE

Incised & sculpted pot "books"
n.b. POT CARRIER who goes
forgetfully between worlds
in Navajo myth

& contemporary POT BOILERS
or "source of livelihood"

Campbell
L-854

3 decades later the comp
list for THE MYTHIC IMAGE
shows copies sent to
150 addresses including:
  Alan Watts
  Eliade
  J. Kitagawa
  Stan Grof
  Rollo May
  Jean Houston
  Carl Schorske
  Wm. McGuire
  Maud Oakes
  the Mellons
  Kristine Mann Library
  many Libraries
  Ru Ritsema
  Michael Fordham
  Aniela Jaffe

after illus. de Robart Fuzier

Q: of the value of the image SPRING 52 published
     excerpt but I doubt they published the
     drawings by Belgian master cartoonist.
     Images for my Duncan piece came out
     poorly. To be fair, it used to be very ex-
     pensive to publish artwork. But a SPRING
     editor told me, "we never publish poetry."
     Is picture-writing in the same category—
     especially the cartoon?

This book by Ander Monson is so new it's not
catalogued yet. Right at the start he writes:
" To archive is political. To keep a story on
  a shelf or to remember then retell it
  means it will be more likely to exist.
  after we have gone. It will all be gone
  in time. Maybe this is the best we can
  do." p4 LETTER TO A FUTURE LOVER (2015)
    Marginalia, Errata, Secrets, Inscriptions
    and other Ephemera Found in Libraries

Figure 3 Nor Hall, Day Page 6. OPUS Archives, Pacifica Graduate Institute.

PART II:

THE THEORETICAL IMPORTANCE OF SENEX & PUER IN ARCHETYPAL PSYCHOLOGY: FOUNDATION AND EXTENSIONS

Glen Slater, Ph.D., has studied and trained in religious studies and clinical psychology. For the past eighteen years he has taught Jungian and archetypal psychology at Pacifica Graduate Institute, where he is a professor in the depth psychology programs. He edited and introduced the third volume of James Hillman's *Uniform Edition, Senex & Puer,* as well as a volume of essays by Pacifica faculty, *Varieties of Mythic Experience,* and has contributed a number of essays to Jungian journals and collections. He is writing a book on technologism, the psychology of the posthuman movement and related implications for living in the Digital Age.

GLEN SLATER

Hillman's Metapsychology

"THERE IS NOTHING that does not belong to one God or another" (Hillman, 1975, p. 169). James Hillman's half-century of psychological writings, which deeply engaged many archetypal patterns, was shaped by one archetypal configuration in particular—senex and puer. When his engagement with these figures first surfaced at Eranos in 1967, he was embroiled in a struggle with the old guard in Zurich, reading the air of the culture in Europe and in America, and evidently waging an inner battle about where to adopt and where to challenge the depth psychological field in which he was now fully immersed. Hillman (2005) began that seminal paper with Jung's reference to living in the *kairos*, a "unique moment of transition in world history" (p. 31) where there is a "metamorphosis of the gods" (p. 30). He goes on to describe this moment in terms of a "struggle with the psychological connections between past and present, old and new, expressed archetypally as the polarity of senex and puer" (p. 31). Hillman's oeuvre, which took on greater momentum following the gathering of these insights, may be viewed as an ongoing overcoming of this polarity, and in what follows I want to set out some implications of this view.

That paper, "Senex and Puer: An Aspect of the Historical and Psychological Present," described the problem of individuation landing upon a younger generation. He writes of "the 'puer problem'" as a "collective neurosis . . . a psychic expression of an historical claim, and as such is a call" (p. 37). Here he's reframing the psychology of the puer, moving the gravity away from personal psychodynamics and towards archetypal and collective significances. He takes Marie-Louise von Franz's view of the puer personality as being mother-bound and instead sees the regression of psychic energy into the unconscious as the result of the breakdown of traditional structures, forcing youth on a search for meaning when external authority and direction lose their veracity. The puer problem is thus viewed as a symptom of the times; it stems from a collective, historical failure to hold together past and present, old and new. As Hillman saw it, the failure of the elders created the brooding, youthful soul-searching and flights of imagination, leading to a countercultural movement. And the question that still needs to be taken up, not only by the puer personality but by all of us at the turn of the millennium, is how to reconnect the present and the past in a way that once again allows psychic energy and the imagination to flow.

This is the spirit in which Hillman (2005) refers to "us" as "makeweights that may tip the scales of history" (p. 31)—taking another cue from Jung. Clearly he saw himself as such a makeweight, and his character and calling are aligned in this recognition with a perceived shift in the collective psyche. Archetypal psychology begins here, right where the individual complex, forging a personal destiny, is met by the stage of history. Hillman himself tells us this: at the beginning of *The Myth of Analysis* (1972), writing that the manuscript grew out of and around his work on the puer; in the preface to *Re-visioning Psychology* (1992), where he cites his "immersion in a book on the Puer" and writes about "a prolonged and still incomplete defense of my traits and behaviors" (p. xiii); and all the way to *The Soul's Code* (1996), where he says his "acorn theory . . . seems to have sprung from and to speak the language of the *puer eternus*" (p. 311). Yet the senex is also there—in the depth, dedication, and consistency evident in these writings and in the turn to the past, particularly to the Greek and Neoplatonic traditions. *The Myth of Analysis*, which attempts to put depth psychology on a different archetypal footing, begins with a senex question: what fathers psychology? The senex is in the attempt to tie new ideas with old ones, in the very grind of the scholarly process and, as Hillman once told me, in the "heavy artillery" of ancient sources, intellectual authorities, and traditional wisdom, evident in the copious footnotes of these otherwise spritely works.

I've called this piece "Hillman's Metapsychology" in order to recover and name a primary stream of thought, an arch-perspective. This is a move of consolidation aimed at describing a core value and get beneath the basic question of what Hillman is doing: a psychology of psychology? A therapy of ideas? A cultivation of imagination? Loving gods and fighting Titans? Returning soul to the world? What is behind or within each of these things? What is the hidden monotheism in all the polytheism? One answer concerns the reconciliation of these archetypal figures, senex and puer, into what he called the *union of sames*.

From these early writings on, in every essay, book, and lecture, Hillman aimed to overcome the polarizing tendency of this archetypal pairing and work towards their confluence. He did this by remembering the gods in all things, knowing that the new was doomed without recalling the old, and the old was dead without reentering the new. As many of us found out the hard way, both the outworn adage and the New Age ideal found their way to his chopping block; he disliked clichés just as much as fads. For a short time in the nineties these antipathies even landed upon the word "soul," which otherwise occupied a core position in his rhetoric. Yet when it was losing its imaginative chops and finding a home in car commercials and magazine ads he pulled back for a while. Hillman was iconoclastic, which can be a puer trait, but the smashing of idols was always for a deeper purpose, in order to get us out of our intellectual recliners and move a bit, and in the moving, find *psyche* rather than just mind and *imagination* rather than just knowledge.

In order to appreciate this consistency in the diverse range of topics and styles Hillman engages, we must learn to grasp the senex aspects of his approach, which can be less apparent amidst the flashes of insight and mythic flourishes. We must sometimes follow him in the direction of formality and the discussion of psychic structures and dynamics. He suggests, for instance, *"this specific archetype will be involved in the process character of any complex"* (2005, p. 36; emphasis in original). Here he's following Jung's royal road; if work on the psyche is first a work on complexes, and if they are the configurations by which the many archetypes come into life, then the senex-puer relationship might be said to pave this path into the depths. The polarization of this relationship is grounds for the complex preserving its tightly wound grip on us, and the reconciliation of the relationship accompanies the release of the complex's creative potential. Hillman writes, for example, "complexes can cloud themselves with puer-illusions" and "senex-consciousness penetrates these illusions with its fantasy of 'bitter truth,'" which also "turns into a life-style of permanent cynicism for all complexes, the seeing through of everything" (p. 254). Neither endless fantasizing nor dry intellectual principles will loosen a complex. He also argues, "the most recalcitrant encrustations of the complex, its oldest habits . . . are neither childhood remnants nor parental introjections, but senex phenomena, that is, *the structure and principles by which the complex endures"* (p. 274). On the other side, "the puer personifies the moist spark within any complex or attitude that is the original dynamic seed of spirit . . . It is . . . the call of a person to his or her daimon" (p. 54). This suggests the telos of the complex, its purposefulness, belongs to the puer. Yet the moist sparks of any complex so often need what he refers to as a "working on Saturn, a depressive grinding" that is therapy (p. 274) in order to be released. Perhaps we could sum up these insights by saying an archetypal psychotherapy's senex aspect appears in the regressive, repetitive, and restrictive nature of the process, its containment, boundaries, and tiresome work. And the puer aspect comes with the play, the spiritual release and the moments of grace. The union of sames thus corresponds to the individuation of the complex and the revelation of its daimonic aspect and full archetypal significance. What these insights convey is Hillman's sense of the senex and puer imbedded in both the essential nature of the complex and in our approaches to it, and the union of sames taking place when the complex releases its creative potential and settles into our deeper character.

Beyond these excursions into psychodynamics, Hillman's is mainly a psychology of perspective, of imagination, rooted in understanding the archetypes themselves as ways of imagining or, as Jung (1960a) said, "modes of apprehension" (p. 136 [par. 277]). And in generating an archetypal perspective on contemporary concerns and events we can also see the way in which the union of sames—the overlap of past, present, and future in the psyche—is pervasive. This psychology of perspective was there in his first book, the encyclopedic study *Emotion* (1960), where he puts forth the idea that "explanatory and therapeutic psychology . . . are enmeshed with each other" (p. 287). In other words, we're doing therapy when we're doing theory. It is this collapse of idea and action that is also at the heart of his notion of psychologizing: seeing through literal realities to their metaphorical and archetypal import, releasing an idea buried in an action, or recognizing the active force of an idea. "Dissolving the problem into the fantasy that is congealed into a 'problem'" (1975, p. 135) and "the *epistrophé* or reversion through likeness of an event to its mythical pattern" (1997, p. 47) become the essential maneuvers in this perspective, which reunites an immediate phenomenon or notion with its timeless, universal psychic roots—the old and the new.

Sometimes superficial encounters with Hillman's work result in an impression of intellectualization, puer cleverness and slipperiness, and a lack of concern for affect and embodied experience. But this reaction often evidences a failure to understand the mutual fertilization of thoughts and images that runs through his writings; emotion, body, relationship, and experience are never far away in archetypal psychology, as long as the bonds of thinking and imagination are maintained. Yet thinking imaginatively requires a range of thought, a repertoire of ideas, gathered from a number of fields and different ages, reflecting a disciplined scholarship combined with a love of words, stories, and metaphor. Here, it's not the idea itself, but the way it is handled and applied that counts. Here, in the very weaving and working of ideas, we find both a heavy arsenal and a light touch. Here, we find the union of sames inhabiting his style of doing psychology.

It is this union of sames that Hillman (1972) brings to what he called "applying psychology to psychology" (p. 40). In tracking the fantasies, images, and archetypal patterns at work in theory, especially in Jungian theory, we witness a deliberate challenge to convention and authority, an undoing of fixed ideas. To put an idea into therapy, you must first be able to imagine historical complexes and parental lineage; that is, have an eye for unconscious foundations, looking for where the idea is anchored in ancient forms and ancestral threads. This brings movement and vitality to reification and abstraction. The looking back is done in the spirit of moving forward, in search of a more substantial psychic ground.

Dissolving theories into fantasies and fantasies into images means taking a stand with the old man. Yet these challenges and stands will leave the ground of significance and be merely rebellious unless they are in service to deeper principles. The very term "archetypal imagination," which works towards seeing gods in all things, is a union of sames, uniting the immediate and particular with the timeless and universal. In other words, the new image or the revealed idea that comes from seeing through the theory has to be grounded in instinct, in service to the ancient rhythms of life. The senex concern with authority is also a concern with that which *authors*. It returns us to history, philosophical antecedents, and traditional wisdom.

As Hillman came to prominence, however, more classical Jungians saw only flight and rebellion, which is how the puer looks from a senex perspective. The critics returned to the theme because, as I argued at the 2000 "Psychology at the Threshold" conference in Santa Barbara (pp. 205ff.), what was most apparent in the archetypal approach was the iconoclasm and heterodoxy, the *via negativa*, while all the heavy artillery and philosophical anchorage in the footnotes were pushed to the margins. Hillman wasn't interested in the kind of systematic or hierarchical thought that would combat these charges. Failing to bring these more foundational elements of the project to the surface, the archetypal approach could also sometimes invite its own negative senex, right in the midst of its concerns with imaginal vitality—a dogmatic embrace of fluidity, a deconstructive imperative, a monotheistic polytheism. Among some followers, the poetic flourish and clever deconstructions appeared to promote a lack of discipline or continuity—an imaginative dance without grounding in some intellectual tradition or prior knowledge of Jung. This negative senex shadow was acknowledged by Hillman after the 1992 Notre Dame conference. He commented then on "the fanatic devotion to single agendas," pointing out that "monotheism appears within psychological polytheism as contentious demands and intrusive invasions" (qtd. in Tacey, 1998, p. 231). "Theories too are afflicted with shadow" (p. 285), he wrote at the end of *The Soul's Code*, in the same place noting that puer-based theories have "a show-off aestheticism . . . but forgo the labors of proof" (p. 283).

Nonetheless, one antidote to this senex shadow rising from a puer emphasis, whereby the senex is more consciously courted, is to be found right there in the writings. The puer must marry the psyche, as he put it in "Peaks and Vales" (2005, pp. 71ff.), and he parallels this marriage with that of Eros and Psyche, where psychological becoming is through love, and with *Mysterium Coniunctionis* (Jung, 1960b), where it is spirit and matter that must find their connection. As he further specifies, it is "the mess of psyche," its "perplexity" that the puer needs to join. The soaring spirit must bed the madness. The puer, the spirit, the peak needs the anima, the soul, the vale. This is the way of depth, not only wedding psychological theory to psychopathology but also wedding insights to the history of ideas and mythic forms. It is this fidelity to the underworld rather than to upper world systems and principles that also makes archetypal psychology a looser, scrappier undertaking.

The *Uniform Edition* of Hillman's writings is one place where the "loose ends" are collected, however; where there's a fantasy of consolidation at work, and where we might be invited to grasp a few threads, or locate a few more "fenceposts," as he called them in *Re-visioning Psychology* (1975). It is itself a senex nod to the disjointed, puer-inspired, many and varied writings of James Hillman—*puer-et-senex*. As I wrote in the introduction to *Senex & Puer*, I think that Hillman's work in this area "may be regarded as an arterial expression" of the field (p. xv). If *Re-visioning Psychology* is the text, these essays, which gather around this archetypal configuration, are the subtext, conveying the place within the field, and the place within the history of ideas, that Hillman came to occupy.

We still live in a time in which the polarization of this archetypal configuration dominates. Two of the three major quotes with which Hillman opens the *Senex & Puer* papers concern the challenges technology poses for the psyche. Jung underscores the need to account for the moment of kairos, "if humanity is not to destroy itself through the might of its own technology and science," and Hoyle writes of our having "no real contact with the forces that are shaping the future" (p. 30). In the Information Age, with its adoption of technological-solutionism, the new has all but abandoned the old, and across the globe the old is staging a desperate, destructive, regressive retribution in all forms of fundamentalism. The increased speed of information exchange and its colossal accumulation cannot address the continual cry for meaning, purpose, and identity. As posthumanists imagine ways to depart from the earthly and organic processes of existence, environmentalists are calling us back to a simpler time. The polarization remains. In hearing once again this base note of Hillman's thought, perhaps we might see where and how we might still be makeweights.

"From these early writings on, in every essay, book,

and lecture, Hillman aimed to overcome the polarizing tendency

of this archetypal pairing and work towards their confluence.

He did this by remembering the gods in all things,

knowing that the new was doomed without recalling the old,

and the old was dead without

reentering the new."

—Glen Slater

Rodney C. Teague, Ph.D., recently relocated with his wife, Erin Leigh, sons Tal and Ches, and daughter Emma Ruby to the south Dallas suburb of Cedar Hill. He works at the Dallas VA Medical Center to promote a highly contextual and personalized approach to mental wellness among military veterans and their families. Teague earned a doctoral degree in Clinical Psychology from Duquesne University. While at Duquesne—and previously at the University of Dallas—he studied psychology as a human science from existential, phenomenological, and critical perspectives. He came to psychology initially through literature—through Faulkner, Dostoevsky, and Shakespeare viewed in light of a collective (un)conscious, and he continues to make his way back to and through literature. Mentors at the University of Dallas, the Dallas Institute, and Duquesne University nurtured—and go on nurturing—this trajectory. Currently, his clinical work is with veterans who are diagnosed with mental illness, addictions, and who have had experiences of combat and other trauma. This work connects him to his late grandfathers, both decorated World War II veterans. It also connects him with the vast capacity of the human soul for suffering and resilience. Existential and narrative perspectives inform his work.

Archetypal Thinking as Imaginal Practice

THE SENEX-PUER assemblage is foundational for an archetypal perspective be-cause it demonstrates one of James Hillman's primary discoveries regarding the operation of psyche: that psyche is not populated by static archetypal figures with proper names and personalities. Rather, it is characterized by activities and movements—asymmetrical and generative—that are archetypal. His exploration of senex-puer dynamism draws attention—by contrast—to a general condition in the human world of psychic and imaginal impoverishment. An archetypal per-spective may potentially breathe life and warmth into this predicament. James Hillman's explorations and, I hope, our continuing discussions are, then, attempts to enhance our collective ability to participate imaginatively in the world.

In the opening essay of the work under present consideration, the con-stellation of the puer-senex polarity as "split" denotes no less than an historical crisis (2005, p. 32). The attitudinal opposition of old and young typifies rigid, literal, and impoverished psychic participation—poor imagining—increasingly evident in our data-driven monoculture. In fact, this opposition is itself an example of split-senex sensibility: inflexible and stale. The result is immoderate, unbalanced, and inelegant—characterized by fascistic rigidity on the split-senex side and reactionary idealization and idolization of youth on the other (split-puer).

Hillman (2005) describes this formula using the example of conscious-ness that has tended to be described as either "good" or "bad" with ascription of the opposite sign to the unconscious. "This tendency works for every pair of opposites," he states, "[t]he view and value we have of one pair of a polarity is taken from within the standpoint of the other . . . we can never be wholly outside our own consciousness" (p. 35). It is no wonder Hillman nods to Lao Tzu (1988), the "old master," whose wisdom, collected as the *Tao-te-ching*, elucidates the harmonious interplay of seeming opposites and the folly of false polarity. "When people see some things as beautiful, other things become ugly. . . . Long and short define one another. High and low depend on one another" (p. 2). In the best rendering of their archetypal formulation, senex and puer define and depend on one another. Through the "way of ambivalence," holding dearly to paradox (p. 40), we may apprehend and be healed by the dynamic nature of their operation.

But ego, uneasy with ambivalence and wearing but "one face at a time" (Hillman, 2005, p. 35), imposes its value judgments upon polarity. This ego, cast here as perpetrator of the split, has itself been truncated and dismembered, divorced from psyche. This ego's world-narrowing "disjunctive rationalism" (p. 36) is part of what Hillman describes in his essay, "On Psychological Language"

(1960) as an extended campaign to colonize the unconsciousness (psyche/soul/ imagination) by a "reality coping ego consciousness" (p. 184) bent on claiming that dark territory in the name of the progress. Hillman argues that the Enlightenment identification of ego with rational development relegated psyche, with her ambiguities, to a marginal and defensive position. Insistence on the literal, concrete, on "one or the other" rather than "both, and" is an attempt to foreclose ambivalence, paradox, and syncretic entailment. This stance characterizes a culture that relegates imagination to youth and insists that, by maturity, its adherents accept the parenthetical "merely" that precedes any instance of "imaginal," "imaginary," or any other explicit imputation of psyche's activities into language. Development understood as the linear march of progress has no place for the ambiguities and circularities of soul. They must be excised.

It is precisely against this rationalist/imperialist onslaught that Jung's work appears. By "training" consciousness to think symbolically (psychologically), Jung aimed to heal the split ego. Hillman (1960) calls this the development of "imaginal ego," and his own archetypal work continues the restoration of harmony to imagination, ego, soul and consciousness (p. 183). It is this rift—ego identified with rational cogito and estranged from soul—to which Hillman (2005) refers as the "fundamental split" and the "main work" of analysis (p. 35). His explication of the senex-puer archetype inspires continuing explorations in this vein and the work represents Hillman's faithful efforts to renew our awareness of the schism afflicting us and to thereby renew possibilities for healing.

This work proceeds because the archetypes and the activities of psyche are characterized by paradox and ambivalence (2005, p. 34ff.). Hillman describes the polarity of senex and puer as "potential." That we speak of them separately is heuristic—drawing our attention, ultimately, to their *coniunctio*. Consideration of their asymmetrical dynamism drives a hermeneutic perspective—a style of being in and imagining in the world that is by turns participatory and reflective. This "way of ambivalence" suggests that we should listen to the world with duplicitous "Hermetic" ears that hear multiple modes simultaneously. We should perceive boundaries (or contradictions) that spring up between seeming opposites as thresholds for crossing rather than censorious obstacles (2005, p. 95ff.). Hermetic awareness holds the tension of in-between, allowing room for us to operate—and to play—with the real.

Rapprochement "in order to heal a fundamental split" between senex and puer—what Hillman (2005) describes as the "main work of psychoanalysis" (p. 39)—requires harmonization of senex-puer sensibilities. One works toward harmony through increasing awareness of the operations and activities of senex-puer and by practicing the way of ambivalence, holding the tension of paradox. This is the work of cultivating imaginal ego. We wrestle with the impossibility of easy categorization into boxes labeled "youth" and "old age," "innovation," or "stagnation." Confronted with the questions of technology, we can ignore neither the tantalizing moist spark of creative eruptions nor the world-effacing monolith of "big data." Like the senex-puer archetype as described in its am-bivalent wholeness, imaginal ego is discontinuous, uroboric; "a circulation of the light and the darkness" (1960, p. 184). As we contend with archetypal paradox, we gain familiarity with "psychic reality," understood as the imaginal world, with an ultimate aim of more faithfully imagining the real (p. 185).

In "On Psychological Language," Hillman specifically addresses the function of analysis with respect to pathology. I am reading the exploration of the senex-puer archetype as cultural therapeutic that may serve much the same function. Through its encounter with the circuity of psychic action, the "I" is "drawn into the halls of memoria, becoming itself but one more of the particulars that finds its place in association with an archetype" (1960, p. 186). Imaginal ego is culti-vated—ego finds its rightful place—as a consequence of butting up against the limitations of the rationalist-positivist ego and through reflection upon resulting conundrums. "Though imagination seems to be inside me, as a faculty of my soul, it is also possible to experience myself inside the imaginal, where the ego is no longer an independent factor, carrying consciousness like a lamp or knife..." (p. 186).

Does imagination belong to senex or puer? Of course not! Roughly put, the whole world is imaginal. We are—willing or not—passengers on its course. The archetypal *perspective* is just that—radically perspectival. The meaning of things at any given moment depends largely on one's point of view. Glen Slater (2005) puts this succinctly in the introduction to the *Senex & Puer* volume: "there is no neutral standpoint, only looking from one psychological place to another" (p. xxii). This is Jung's call for consciousness to think psychologically, just as it is the Hermetic (and hermeneutic) stance to which Hillman calls us.

Methodological hermeneutics as derived from Husserl's phenomenolo-gy accords with the cultivation of imaginal ego as described here. Its foundation is an understanding that phenomena—texts, human activities, etc.—require in-terpretation because their meanings are multivocal and polysemous. But it also posits that we must move with facility between modes of engagement—from pre-reflective participation in the world to a less embedded observer-state of reflection and interpretation (Packer, 1985, p. 1086). Hillman (1960) is suggesting a kind of imaginal hermeneutics when he writes "we need a new way of looking, an imaginative way, a way that starts from within the imaginal itself, so that ev-erything we look at becomes an example" (p. 201), and again, "the imaginal proj-ects us into participation with the phenomena they tell us about. . . . By shifting the position of consciousness. . . . we view the so-called factual from the archetypal" (p. 202). Then, in the work under present consideration, Hillman summarizes the importance of senex-puer for cultivating meaning in the shift toward imaginal ego: "Meaning expresses the invisible coincidence of the positive puer with the positive senex" (p. 54). And finally,

> In answering one's own question one is *puer-et-senex*. In questioning one's own answer one is *senex-et-puer.* The two faces turned towards each other in dialogue. This unending dialogue with oneself and between oneself and the world is that which holds one in meaning. (p. 64)

With respect to imagination, we readily posit a primary role for puer as the innovative, creative, effacing, dissolving force for de-formation. However, we are also in imagination as structure, and that is a senex aspect. His is the codification of imagination, tending "to concretize [his] perspective as 'real,' 'hard,' and 'out there'" (2005, p. 324). This aspect tends toward Saturnine rigidity but is also prerequisite for any experience of meaningfulness. But we know better than to believe the propaganda of a reified and contentious split. The goal for adaptation of the imaginal ego is no less than imagining reality. We imagine from within the imaginal. Hillman (1960) writes, "we never cease projecting. We are dreaming all the time" (p. 177). Maurice Merleau-Ponty (1945) describes the "real" as "a closely woven fabric" resulting from a creative act of reflection upon an unreflective experience (p. xi). Through his deep exploration of the puer-senex archetype, Hillman creates the conditions—mythic ambivalence and paradox—for the cultivation of an interpretive consciousness. We are invited to train ourselves to *imagine better* through archetypal interpretation.

I'll close with an analogy to the vital but overlooked activity of breathing. Here is an automatic even "autonomic" function, necessary to sustaining life but which we can largely ignore and which we tend to take entirely for granted. Without a moment's thought or conscious effort given to breathing, one can proceed from the moment of birth to the moment of death with little noticeable *deficiency*. However, we know from yogis, monks, athletes, altos and laboring mothers that we can intentionally direct awareness to our breathing and then learn to breathe differently. And we know that changing our breathing can change our health, performance, experience of pain, etc. The analogy to imagination has to do with how we participate in the world, psyche and imagination. Like breathing, we do it from cradle to grave. And we can get by with very little thought to how we participate in weaving the fabric of our reality. The natural attitude tells us that imagination is internal, personal and fleeting—mere kid stuff. However, with careful attention to our perspectives we may enhance our awareness of the divisions that impoverish us, change our relationship to a meaningful world and, as Hillman wrote, heal.

But the conceit is more textured than simply that. Breathing re-training may be undertaken as a behavioral intervention with an instrumental aim of pain relief, performance improvement, or improved blood oxygen saturation. These take part in a useful but limited materialist view of respiration and nervous system function. Medical and therapeutic knowledge around these operations are ruled by senex accretion. "Yes, yes," it is said, "we know how all that works." However, imagine what happens when I undertake to breathe differently. First, I gain awareness of what was previously sub-liminal. Puer's spark reveals something novel in what had been carefully and invisibly curated. I learn that I have somehow been estranged from this most basic activity of living. And now I learn that I can participate actively in the process. And when I do participate differently, my experience of myself changes as a consequence.

Now conscious of what was hidden, breathing becomes an interpenetrating participation between the world and me. Rhythmically, I take the world's atmosphere into my physical interior and then expel bits of myself into the world's "great lung" (Merleau-Ponty, 1945, p. 246). Puer characterizes inspiration / inhalation while senex presides over the continual dying and renewal of drawing and holding one's breath. He holds greedily, loath to relinquish his prize until, burning and depleted, he sighs deeply. A shift in consciousness—here, about breathing, which demonstrates a dawning awareness of a previously hidden split—heals.

Paradox draws consciousness off its track, initiating a shift. When I pay attention to what happens when I breathe, I am confronted by a mystery. I thought I was me, enclosed and self-sufficient. But at every moment I admit the outside into me and I turn my inside out and give it to the air about me. In time I gain familiarity with this experience of breathing. I come to appreciate the process and the paradox. All the "I's" are drawn into something larger and mysterious. Effort-borne awareness around a fundamental division potentiates healing.

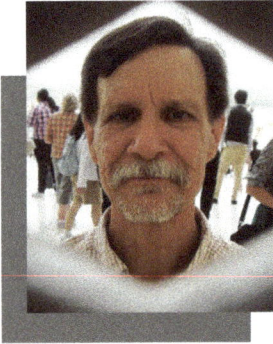

Tom Cheetham, Ph.D., is a biologist and philosopher and the author of four books on the imagination and the meaning of Henry Corbin's work for the contemporary world, most recently *All the World An Icon: Henry Corbin and the Angelic Function of Beings* (2012). He complied the bibliography of Archetypal Psychology for James Hillman's *Archetypal Psychology: A Brief Account*. He is a Fellow of the Temenos Academy in London and Adjunct Professor of Human Ecology at the College of the Atlantic in Bar Harbor, Maine. He lectures regularly in Europe and the U.S.

TOM CHEETHAM

Errands to an Adjoining Zone

The spry Arms of the Wind
If I could crawl between
I have an errand imminent
To an adjoining Zone —

—Emily Dickinson (1864)

ACCORDING TO HIS long-time friend Denis de Rougemont (1981), a young and passionate Henry Corbin once playfully echoed the revolutionary Marxists with his own call to arms, "Heretics of the world unite!" (p. 298). Recalling this anecdote as an old man, Corbin said that no, he certainly would not have said "heretics," but rather "esotericists." I trust de Rougemont's memory. The cautious conservatism of Corbin's later years is also evident in his displeasure with James Hillman's appropriation of his carefully chosen neologism, the *mundus imaginalis*, or the imaginal world, as a translation of the Arabic *'alam al-mithal*. But Corbin had himself adopted many of his central notions from the Shi'ites and applied them far beyond their original context across the Abrahamic religions as a whole. Not a few scholars have critiqued him for interpreting all of Islam through an exclusively Shi'ite lens. And he was often criticized for his rampant eclecticism and disregard for the strictures of historical scholarship. He happily transgressed geographic and temporal boundaries in the pursuit of an ecumenical and all-embracing vision of religious harmony. It should have been no surprise to him that his grand project of a general "comparative spiritual hermeneutics" would inevitably produce the creative and unpredictable hermeneutic metamorphoses that occur whenever cultures interact.

The central pillar of Corbin's psychocosmology is the act of spiritual transformation known in Arabic as *ta'wil*. *Ta'wil* is spiritual hermeneutics, and is, he says (2003), "the mainspring of *every* spirituality" (p. 28; my emphasis). *Ta'wil* is the interpretation of a text or of the world read as a text, which acts as an alchemical elixir for the human soul. It is an interiorization of meaning that transforms by means of the energies of the creative imagination. In Corbin's theology this supreme act of imagination is the perfection of prayer. James Hillman and his colleagues enthusiastically adopted the *ta'wil* along with the *mundus imaginalis* and integrated them into depth psychology. Many radical poets, especially in the U.S., found Corbin's work to be a revelation, a celebration, and affirmation of the power and beauty of the imagination, and they adapted the *ta'wil* as the key to the exercise of the properly creative imagination.

The ontology that underlies *ta'wil* for Corbin is a duality between the earthly soul and its heavenly Twin, who is the Angel Out Ahead, bestower of creative power and guarantor of mystic ascent. The grammar of the language through which God breathes beings into existence—the grammar that governs Creation—depends upon the middle voice. Every verb, Corbin says, is conjugated in the middle voice. Every action is in reality both action and passion. In the active voice the subject acts; in the passive, is acted upon; in the middle voice the subject *both acts and is acted upon*. We speak and are spoken by our Angel. The middle voice is, in the words of the composer Stefan Wolpe, "what makes music work" (qtd. in Butterick, 1980, p. 59). Corbin said as a young man, "the rhythm of music is the rhythm of my soul" (qtd. in Cheetham, 2015). The fundamental harmonies that structure the world are expressions of the counterpoint between earthly beings and their heavenly twins. The grand symphony of this harmonic cosmology depends on the cyclical structure of eternal time, of which linear, historical time is a feeble and fallen image. The manifestation of any of the myriad beings in Creation can only occur as the result of such a rhythmic counterpoint between the heavenly and earthly poles of a person—only in this dialogue can beings emerge from the depths of their hiddenness and become Present. The Greek verb for this display, conjugated in the middle voice to express the syzygy, the circumincession of persons, is *apophanesthai*. The *apophanesthai* necessary for beings to be revealed in their unhiddenness is the highest act of creative imagination. That is how living reality is disclosed. Only by means of the creative energies released by the interplay of the divine and the earthly can idols be dissolved and released towards their truth: all beings have a secret angelic function as icons, windows on the infinite worlds beyond. All fixed realities only seem so to the literal mind, and, as Hillman so often pointed out, the literal is only one mode of imagining. Hermes, translator of the gods, dissolves the boundaries of the literal, and the worlds of the imaginal are opened by the *ta'wil*, the hermeneutics of the spirit. Your autonomy is a fiction, Corbin says. The world in which you live is a representation of the state of your soul. You and your world are the thought of the Angel, thought through and with you. To keep this wonderful dance in eternal motion, Corbin (2003) calls for a "permanent hermeneutics" (p. 142).

These are the gifts Corbin gave us. But there can be no predicting where a hermeneutics of the imagination will lead. Emerson said that the imagination flows, and never freezes. Corbin gave us a cosmology of the imagination, but as an old man he wanted to keep it trapped in the mystical Persian vessel in which he delivered it. The *ta'wil* of course escaped, and the stories of its further adventures are great dramas of creative imagination. It escaped into archetypal psychology but also, even more wildly, into poetry.

In a lecture delivered in Buffalo in 1983 for the Analytical Psychology Society of Western New York, the poet Robert Duncan spoke about Hillman's work. He said Hillman wanted it both ways. He wanted a poetic psychology. But Duncan warned that it isn't possible. Poetry and science don't mix. He said that Hillman talks as if he was doing psychology, but he never produces any evidence! Duncan is a bit harsh, and Hillman often managed to straddle the divide, I think, but Duncan was absolutely right that there is a critical difference between the imagination as it operates in art and poetry, in the wilds of the psyche so to speak, and as it operates at the meta-level of archetypal psychology. Duncan felt this most forcefully in Hillman's alchemical writings. In these Duncan thought Hillman very nearly breaks into poetry. Speaking of "Alchemical Blue and the Unio Mentalis," Duncan (1996) said, "it seems to me . . . [this] is the place where I find my goodness, aren't you in trouble, Hillman, because you have entered very close to the poem in what you are doing" (p. 35). Why trouble? Because poetry breaks the frame. You're no longer in the walled City, but in the Wilderness—not talking *about* the gods, but inviting them to act through you. *Ta'wil* in action. This is the territory of what Corbin called the *récit*, the visionary recital. The poet Robert Kelly (1974), who has long drawn on Corbin's work, calls them "endless, beautiful stories that spill themselves out of uncertain meaning," the kind of fable that cannot be paraphrased, and that is the alchemical operation in action. The recital isn't *about* anything; it is the thing itself. We are in the realm of unknowing. Or better, as Duncan (1996) puts it, neither knowing nor not knowing is involved. He says believing and imagining are part of different systems: "While you're imagining you can't believe or disbelieve. Imagination crosses out all this business of knowing and not knowing. When you get news in the imagination it doesn't [bother you whether you] know it or do not know it" (p. 4).

This is why Hillman was "in trouble"; this is risky business. Imagination flows, and to flow with it you have to be open, perched on the edge of chaos, able to hold on to nothing at all. At it's most challenging, the imagination can require that we live on the knife edge of nonsense that we may push towards the temporarily meaningless in order to move into new landscapes of meaning and feeling (Varnedoe, 2006, p. 271). This is what it's like to be in the grip of Hermes Mercurius.

In an essay on Frank O'Hara's art criticism, John Yau (2006) illuminates the crucial distance between the ordering principles that govern theory and the unruly energies of creative imagination:

> O'Hara's critical stance runs counter to what many believe an art critic, curator, or, more recently, cultural theorist should do, which is *possess and continually refine a set of standards which is brought to bear on the situation*. By contrast, O'Hara felt that the viewer must always be alert in a reality that is contingent and constantly

changing. Literally speaking, he has no fixed paradigm, no previously established model by which to judge art... O'Hara makes no distinction between his critical stance and the writing of poetry, where, as he said, "You have to go on your nerve alone." In trying to maintain his openness, O'Hara achieves what Wallace Stevens challenges us all to do: "Live in the world but outside existing conceptions of it." You can't get much more radical than that, or much more exposed. (pp. 6-7; my emphasis)

The radical exposure of such openness is why Hillman is in trouble when he comes close to poetry; the meta-language of psychology begins to break down and give way to something new outside its boundaries. But what lies outside those bounds? Where does the *ta'wil* take us? Another poet with explicit debts to Corbin is Joseph Donahue (2014), who gives us an answer:

I would like to think that my writing practices might come upon possibilities lurking in words and emanating from beyond words. In regard to both structure and theme I tend to think in terms of what Emily Dickinson might call adjoining zones, categories of experience or realms of being that summon us and tend to prioritize the kind of thinking and feeling that goes on in one of these zones. "I have an errand immanent/ to an adjoining zone," she says. Each of those terms—errand, immanent, adjoining and zones—have for many, many years deeply engaged me as a ways of thinking about poetry.... Where are those zones? What awaits there? Who would one be were one to go there and come back?

To practice *ta'wil* is to embark on an errand to these adjoining zones. George Quasha has recently revisited the analysis of *ta'wil* as a poetic adventure that he and Robert Kelly and Charles Stein first engaged in many years ago (Quasha, forthcoming). In his discussion of Kelly's poetic practice he details some salient characteristics of a "poetics of singularity" which are precisely those of Corbin's notion of the recital. The poem is paradoxically both in time and timeless, being an enactment of a continuous present. The reader must engage the poem as if it were her own. The poem is singular because it is primal, an original experience each time it is read. This is because its meaning hovers in perpetual uncertainty; the poem cannot be paraphrased or abstracted; it is irreducible to any scheme or explained by any procedure; it cannot be known in advance and is thus alchemical; the reading is the operation itself; and the event of the poem is an initiatic moment. In a striking image, Kelly has said that the poem builds an Altar, not a Temple. Here is a clue, I think, to where these poets, and Hillman, too, make their break with Corbin. The difference lies in the balance between Altar and Temple. The altar is a place of offering and sacrifice—the altar is open on all sides, exposed, and exceedingly risky. The Temple is the place of worship, and sacrifice as well to be sure, but the sense of enclosure and protection is palpable. Corbin was a passionate champion of the imagination all of his life, but his deeply mystical interiority leads one deep inside the Temple to the heart of beauty and love. He had no feeling whatever for the wild profligacy and the dangerous openness of the arts of modernity. He wrote (1995),

> it is impossible to avoid wondering whether the *mundus imaginalis*, in the proper meaning of the term, would of necessity be lost and leave room only for the imaginary if something like a secularization of the imaginal into the imaginary were not required for the fantastic, the horrible, the monstrous, the macabre, the miserable and the absurd to triumph. On the other hand, the art and imagination of Islamic culture in its traditional form are characterized by the hieratic and the serious, by gravity, stylization and meaning. (p. 20)

As radical as they were in some ways, both Jung and Corbin were frightened by the extremity of the arts and literature of the modern world. For both there were boundaries the imagination must not transgress. These boundaries can become the prison walls of the next generation.

Poetry can save us from ourselves, as Quasha says: "We become fundamentalists of our own constructions." Echoing Corbin's perpetual hermeneutic, Leslie Scalapino calls us to a "perpetual conceptual rebellion" to save ourselves from the "destruction of the world" that is the result of all our dogmas, those frozen relics of once-living thought and feeling that imprison us all. Quasha says that the poem as the *ta'wil* of life returns us to unknowing and openness to reality where "all our secret personal fundamentalisms dissolve into breath." We need to go even further than the young Corbin urged us. Not only should we say, "heretics of the world unite!" More than that we can cry, "Artists and poets of the world, disperse!" With constant alert attention we should not fear living on the edge of chaos, on the knife-edge of nonsense. Go on your nerve! As the great and ill-fated acrobat and tightrope walker Frank Wallenda (2014) said, "Life is on the wire. Everything else is just waiting" (p. 8).

Cheryl Sanders-Sardello (b. 1951–d. 2015), was co-founder and co-director of The School of Spiritual Psychology, in Benson, NC. She was a Fellow of the Dallas Institute of Humanities and Culture, a place she dearly loved. Prior to the founding of The School in 1992, she worked as a counselor of mentally handicapped children, and later as an addictions counselor at Parkland Hospital and Southwestern Medical School in Dallas. At the time of her death, she was writing a book on the healing of the twelve senses in the young and the development of the spiritual senses as we age, with an additional focus on the spiritual psychology of what it means to be in connection with the "so-called dead." By far, Cheryl's most abiding and deep interest was that of learning to enter the process of remaining connected with those who have died and helping others learn to do so. This volume is dedicated to her.

CHERYL SANDERS-SARDELLO

On Being Too Big: Senex-Puer Contemplations

THE THOUGHTS AND ideas in this volume, *Senex & Puer,* are so encyclopedic it makes it hard to "land" anywhere within it; one must be willing to dissolve into the whole even to imagine one can find a single point at the center. Or, maybe within the gathering at the periphery, or the seeking of the center, there is the always being drawn by the opposite, the partner side, seeing extremes, imagining the duality. In order to "see clearly" senex or puer, we attempt to imagine one or the other at a time, to hold each singly up to scrutiny, in an attempt to better understand each on their own standing. However, to stand between senex and puer, one invokes the specter of the other, and neither allows a resting place for imagination without the correlate whirling in. Hillman (2005) states, "puer . . . belongs among the Gods as their vehicle to raise the cosmos to their level. Throughout, the driving force is not aggression or arrogance or potency for its own sake." "The flight upward is in respect to the senex." And, "the deepest desire is not to combat or defeat the senex, since the senex is already darkened and defeated, and, moreover, gains strength by means of darkness and defeat." And later, "it is a spiritual cause; caused by the spirit" (p. 175).

This archetype, these archetypes that spread out around us from this collection, they are so, well, big that they "back" all psychology; they are a foundation for ego. The senex-puer archetype raises the human being out of the simple dualism of body/spirit (that declaration in Constantinople and Nicea).

Soul was lost, dismissed, ignored by choice (as one understanding of the councils) for the sake of generating ego. Ego, as some part of the individual that emerges, can be developed and molded, can mature or remain infantile; grow wise, or be kept childish. Ego is malleable. But soul (that dangerous entity), too, enters the body; experiences the world through the body; watches the ego take hold and learn to think; maneuvers through the lifetime of experiences. Soul founds the love of spirit for the body. Soul is imagined to have hovered about the body and spirit for centuries, held near the archetypal ego and the prototypal spirit by senex-puer aspects. The rhythms of life, the core reality of all being on earth, to be young and exuberant, growing old into wisdom are the simple truths of soul as keystone to incarnation, to duality, to the split of body/spirit.

While senex and puer in mythology become embodied beings, in life they become enacted complexes. Senex and puer become world gestures as political and cultural evolutions. But in the soul, they remain as guides of how to hold together the impossibility of living in ever present paradox. To be incarnated as a spiritual being, we need the mediation of the souls' experience. Senex-puer is the keystone to the bodily knowing self as spirit-soul expression and the spiritual reality of being embedded in matter. Our different psychologies have masked the possibility of balance by being either all about the past or all about the future. Whether officially split by the church, or split by life situations, the split becomes the genesis of pathology, and the place ego becomes trapped. In an ideal world, senex-puer would be balanced, in harmony, in rhythm. Perhaps all psychologies should be based on finding balanced tension—maybe they all are. Nevertheless, the split seems somewhat ingrained, and it encourages radical expressions—even soulless expressions—of one-sidedness. Most recently, this one-sidedness is expressed by exalting in narcissism, encouraging a vacuous adherence to baseless opinions as if they were absolute truths. Where we once looked to our pathologies to find where the gods manifested for modern humanity, we now anesthetize ourselves with mindless newsertainment and assert our interpretational-opinionization rather than seek the truth about anything. (Perhaps one could blame technology.)

We encourage this emptiness in the younger generation, in an attempt to subdue the puer; but then (invoking Dante at the entrance to hell) find ourselves lost in a dark wood of confusion. We may have moved so far away from soul that we verge on losing even the sense of the senex-puer.

In a broader picture, the psychologies of the past (Freudian, Jungian, Adlerian, archetypal) ask: where do you come from? What happened to make you you? Is there an event pivotal to your "you-ness"? What catharsis could alter the past and heal your pain?

The past that can be imagined deeply through memory and memoria. The questions are in the arena of the ego and its ability to reconstruct an accurate representation of the past out of simple memory. The past requires forgiveness, and, for the puer, the past requires justice. Forgiveness seems most likely in the puer universe but is hard to understand, as it is located in the soul as a realm one enters, not an act one does. The will does not forgive. The ego does not forgive. The soul forgives through entering the place of the heart, where forgiveness is a way of being, not an act to be done.

Forgiveness is the very realm in which soul comes to wholeness within one's being in the world, being embodied as individual. Forgiveness expands the soul, becomes the place of the balanced human being.

The future-oriented psychologies—existential, phenomenological, behavioral, cognitive, spiritual—all ask questions about what hasn't happened yet: how do you get to where you want to be? What are you be-coming? How do you create being/behavior? What intuition could open the future to conscious awareness of the "not yet"? How do we perceive the future as being inspired by the unknown to recognize and listen to it? Can the ego perceive the future coming toward it? Does it want to? The future requires freedom. To be open to the unknown, and not be consumed by fear, one must be able to resign the senex-inspired assurances, and be willing to be free of comfortable knowing that assigns meaning and fixes concepts into hard facts. In other words, what if the third principle of thermodynamics is wrong? What if you cannot split the atom any more than you can split the psyche's senex-puer bond?

Hillman (2005) keeps saying, senex-puer is (are) foundational to the ego, and the psychological foundation of the problem of history (p. 35); together, they create the ego's structural components. As previously mentioned, these archetypes "back" all psychologies, ones emerging out of the past, ones leaning toward the future.

When human beings follow a developmental unfolding, what Hillman speaks of as the diversion of the "stages of life," everything psychological becomes encompassed in polarities. At any point in these stages the life of any individual, the archetype of senex-puer is being enacted; soul is being the intermediary (p. 40). Jung observed that moderns were "in search of soul," but senex-puer ensures that soul is always happening within the context of mythologies. Always happening. Like myths. We do not realize we have to have soul to search for soul. Because no matter how cold, hard, and fixed we become, we can still be inspired sometimes, or no matter how flagrantly we soar away, taken over by our passion and joy, we can still be brought back to earth. We are senex-puer through the entirety of life. We are "backed" by the extremes of soul's *raison d'etre*, and almost never just one extreme for too long before the other arises in some fashion, either from within or from without. The point is that senex and puer are (almost) always looking at each other. They define and mock, pressure and tease each other within our psyche, so that we know what we are by seeing what we are not. We determine our own definition of ourselves by pretending that very self is superior to the aspects we condescendingly acknowledge in the other as lesser qualities.

Our culture, most recently, seems to be encouraging the split to greater extremes of pathology and soul-less-ness, perhaps by its insistence that the senex and puer look away from each other, creating a cultural paradox of acceptance of a one-sidedness that leads to addiction and vacuity, maybe even destruction via an "apocalyptic imagination." The result of turning senex and puer away from each other, the splitting off of soul, is the technical human being. The technicalization of everything (beyond the commodification of everything) cripples the development of the prefrontal cortex, eliminating the conscience from the structure of our being.

I began with imagining that senex and puer are too big to speak of in a few moments. They carry too much all-encompassing context and are the foundation of what it means to be a human being. Supposing this is true, the tiny image that they must be held together, not as opposites but as wholeness within a polarity, a deeply rhythmic truth, which makes possible the evolution within our psyche of forgiveness and freedom, is the picture I have attempted to paint for you today.

Forgiveness is the very realm in which soul

comes to wholeness within one's being in the world,

being embodied as individual.

Forgiveness expands the soul, becomes the place

of the balanced human being.

—Cheryl Sanders-Sardello

PART III:

SENEX & PUER REVISIONING IN ART, POETRY, AND CULTURE

Joanne H. Stroud, Ph.D., holds degrees in Psychology and Literature from the University of Dallas, and lectures in Dallas, New York City, and Connecticut. She is a Founding Fellow of the Dallas Institute of Humanities and Culture, Director of Institute Publications, and Editor of the Gaston Bachelard Translation Series, which consists of seven works on elemental imagination written by the French twentieth-century philosopher of science. The 2002 Bachelard Symposium she chaired in Dallas, "Matter, Dream, and Thought," attracted international attention. The series completion in 2011 was celebrated with a Bachelard Day on the 30th anniversary of the Dallas Institute. She served on the Board of Overseers of Harvard University for 12 years and serves on the Boards of the University of Dallas and the Southwestern Medical Foundation currently. She has taught literature and psychology and is author of: *The Bonding of Will and Desire*; the four-volume series *Choose Your Element*: Earth, Air, Fire and Water; and *Time Doesn't Tick Anymore. Gaston Bachelard: An Elemental Reverie on the World's Stuff* and *Towers 2 Tall* were published in 2014.

JOANNE H. STROUD

Poetry Weaves Together the Split
in the Senex-Puer Archetype

IN OUR TIME poetry offers us a singular opportunity to draw together, even to heal the split that Hillman (2005) so aptly describes in the first chapter of this volume, "Senex and Puer: An Aspect of the Historical and Psychological Present." This bizarre suggestion of a way of uniting the cross purposes of conflict between old and new may seem to apply more aptly to the individual personality area than to the cultural background. Nevertheless, I believe that the engagement with great poetry—patiently waiting on the page, or now on a screen, available to one and all, offers a surprisingly strong avenue of amelioration for the fracturing aspect of current culture. The division between past and future, old and new, east and west, and, I would add to this list, liberals and conservatives, Republicans and Democrats, as Hillman emphasizes, all are "expressed archetypally as the polarity of senex and puer" (p. 31). I sense, along with Hillman, that *Kairos*, the right time, is upon us for the metamorphosis of the gods. Hillman made this observation in the period before the advent of the millennium, but it seems even more apt today. The ancient Greek language had two words for designating the different aspects of time—*Cronus*, meaning time as repetition or history, and *Kairos*, which referred to time as lived. Strikingly, both words are senex words, perhaps why we speak of Father Time. Not only in our country but also around the world, polar ideologies rage in anger, war, and destruction against one another. There seems no answer to the ideological splits—between adaptation to modern realities and historically engrained rivalries, between flexible adaptation and rigid, righteous fundamentalism. Any possibility of moving forward is hindered by the unwillingness to consider any compromise, or to admit new ideas. The tearing down of temples and obliteration of artifacts in Syria in an effort to erase the past is testimony to the destructive power of the split polarity.

Hillman's directive to us: *"Therefore our concern must be with archetypal therapy or therapy of an archetype"* (p. 36, my emphasis). What does that mean? I presume that this requires digging down to find common ground shared by both sides before the archetype breaks into differentiation.

All of us are deeply steeped in analytical psychology. It never occurred to me, though, until I read Hillman, that Jungian psychology is so rife with polarities that emphasize the opposites and therefore the split. Hillman reminds us of this direction in Jungian approach: "Jung's life and thought makes more of polarities than does any other major psychological vision. The polar model is basic in all his major psychological ideas" (p. 37). Among other polarizations, Jung posited the Thinking faculty opposite the Feeling, and Sensation opposite to Intuition.

In his excavating efforts, Hillman points out why we are in such a muddle today. There are always tensions; after all, consciousness itself is born in the distinguishing of what is "I" from what is not "I." Why do certain periods in history evidence more extreme examples of polarization? *Why is the center not holding?* (To borrow a line from W. B. Yeats who foresaw this direction.) Hillman attributes the primary cause to the result of three centuries of adherence to the basic Cartesian proposition that emphasized the thinking faculty and ego, or "I," in the famous dictum and tilted Western philosophy toward giving mind dominance over heart wisdom. It was at the time of Descartes that the word "polarity" entered the mainstream and became an issue. Much of the dichotomy we experience now may be the inevitable result of the concentration on the developing and strengthening of the individual ego. With ego development so dominant, we are confronted with its unacknowledged and unwelcome counterpart, with the Shadow—that part of the personality that is so hard for each of us to turn around and see. I always like Robert Bly's image picture of the Shadow, as the body's refusal to reflect, in his *Little Book About the Human Shadow* (1988).

Hillman regards our conscious mind, in which we put our confidence and make our choices, as more often, instead, a block to self-knowledge: "Paradoxically, we are least conscious where we are most conscious. When we are in our ego-efficiency, habitual, feeling most certain, ruling from within that which we know best, we are least reflectively aware" (p. 45). He then adds this wake-up thought: "Out of its own light, the ego makes shadow; the ego is its own shadow; perhaps the ego is shadow" (p. 45). *Perhaps the ego is shadow.* This is a startling assertion. The more light that is shined on the conscious side, the more darkness devours and obscures what is left out or ignored.

Hillman explains that the nature of all Jungian archetypes is an admixture of contraries that can break apart: "The archetype per se is ambivalent and paradoxical, embracing both spirit and nature, psyche and matter, consciousness and unconsciousness; in it the yea and nay are one. . . . The inherent opposition within the archetype splits into poles when it enters ego consciousness. Day breaks with the ego; night is left behind" (p. 38).

Hillman outlines the separate distinctions in this archetype of the senex (related to such words as "Senator" or "senile") and then of the puer (related to the word "puerile") before ultimately returning to the two functionalities as *the union of sames.* It turns out that what we think of as diametrically opposed opposites actually have overlapping similarities if we dig far enough. Surprisingly, for those of us who have worked so hard to strengthen our egos:

> Even the ego's notion of itself as authoritative dominant of consciousness results from the archetypal senex. The Old Wise Man and the Old King are there from the beginning, before the ego is born, governing the mysterious ordering aspect of ego-formation by meaningfully structuring contents into knowledge and extending the area of the will's control. (p. 46)

The assertion in gesture or speech of the demand "I want" or "that's mine" turns out to be an evidence of the senex, even in the earliest life of the baby.

In our culture's admiration of youth and thirst for the ever new, the archetypal senex is generally given a negative flavor. Revealing then that ego development and individuation are also governed by the senex may seem disturbing:

> These qualities—identity of borders, association with consciousness, continuity—we use to describe the ego, and these qualities are each properties of Kronos-Saturn, the senex . . . [E]go-development phenomenon of the senex spirit that works at ordering and hardening within the ego with such compulsion that it must be—as well as the Promethean thrust of the Hero—an instinctual source of ego energy. (p. 47)

We have a tendency to believe that a strong ego can initiate change in any undesirable characteristic, but Hillman says this is a false notion: "Because the negative senex is not an ego fault it cannot be altered by the ego. . . . *These ego problems are consequents rather than causes; they reflect a prior disorder in the archetypal ground of the ego*. The ground is *senex-et-puer*, briefly conceived as its order on one hand, its impetus on the other. Together they give the ego what has been called its *Gestaltungskraft* or intentionality, or meaningfulness of spirit" (p. 47). This attribution of intentionality in the joining of puer to the senex is vital to Hillman and distinguishes his approach from the more usual Jungian one.

Intentionality is such an important impetus. It startles to acknowledge that it is governed by the *senex-et-puer*. Hillman then insists that the only possibility of change emerges in the difficult attempt to put the duality of senex and puer back, Humpty-Dumpty style, together again, no small task. Therefore: "*Our attempt at rapprochement shall go by way of returning to the original condition of the archetype before it has been broken apart and turned against itself*" (p. 39, emphasis in original). Later in the chapter, he enlarges the equal nature of both puer and senex: "As the senex is perfected through time, the puer is primordially perfect. Therefore there is no development, development means devolution, a loss and fall and restriction of possibilities" (p. 52). So, for all its characteristic changeability and flightiness, the puer, like the senex, at its core resists development.

From my point of view, the reading and perhaps even more the learning and reciting of poetry (because then we are more acutely aware of language and its nuances) is efficacious in so many ways—first, it slows us down from the manic pace of contemporary life, causes us to puzzle out and reflect, in short to enter into the presence of another soul personality. It is in the area of soul as opposed to mind that connection is made: speaking psychologically, I'm arguing that one of the hidden pleasures of both poetry and song is the joining together of the senex-puer split, so prevalent in our time.

Poetry, music, and song can be soul satisfying, genuine soul food, the essence of meaning that I believe all of us long for. Hillman agrees:

> The soul itself stands amidst all sorts of opposites as "the third factor." . . . [T]he soul holds polarities in harmony. . . . But now the ego, having replaced the soul as the center of conscious personality, cannot hold the tension. With its destructive rationalism it makes divisions where the soul gives feeling connections and mythic unities. So the soul has come unstrung; its suffering and illness reflect the torn condition of the split archetype. (p. 40)

Is this "third factor" that Hillman ascribes to soul the same as the transcendent factor in Jungian psychology?

I want to include here W. B. Yeats's poem "The Song of Wandering Aengus," one of his early poems that I recited at the 2015 Hillman symposium. A critic has remarked that Yeats wrote in the voice of an old man when he was young and a young man when he was old in true *senex-et-puer* spirit.

> I went out to the hazel wood,
> Because a fire was in my head,
> And cut and peeled a hazel wand,
> And hooked a berry to a thread,
> And when white moths were on the wing,
> And moth-like stars were flickering out,
> I dropped the berry in a stream,
> And caught a little silver trout.
>
> When I had laid in on the floor
> I went to blow the fire aflame,
> But something rustled on the floor,
> And someone called me by my name:
> It had become a glimmering girl
> With apple blossom in her hair
> Who called me by my name
> And faded through the brightening air.
>
> Though I am old with wandering
> Through hollow lands and hilly lands,
> I will find out where she has gone,
> And kiss her lips and take her hands,
> And walk among long dappled grass
> And pluck till time and times are done
> The silver apples of the moon,
> The golden apples of the sun. (p. 60)

In this particular poem, we have youth and age, sun and moon, male and female, temporal time and eternity, the everyday world and the world of myth, all paradoxically juxtaposed. It strains our credulity, but it all works together. The poem also employs vivid alchemical symbolism and bipolar valences. Aengus is a mercurial figure; the quicksilver transforms common matter, making a distillation into precious silver and gold. We remain gathered in the symbolic realm of the tension of opposites. To quote Hillman: "Paradox and symbol express the co-existence of polarity, the fundamental two-headed duality that is both logically absurd and symbolically true . . . by bearing ambivalence one is in the *coniunctio* itself as the tension of opposites. . . . The way is slower, action is hindered, and one fumbles foolishly in the half-light and the symbolic" (p. 41). The key is the bearing of ambivalence.

Also applicable is Robert Sardello's wisdom on the forces at work in lyric poetry:

> It must have to do with the very nature of the creative imagination. That creative imagination makes forms without boundaries, and forms that flow into and around and between and within each other while mysteriously keeping and enhancing clarity by speaking from and to the perceptive organ of the heart. Intellect is not by-passed but with poetry it becomes the servant of the heart, reversing the usual order in which the heart is the servant of the mind.

Poetry connects us not only with the divergences in our own individual psyches, but across the vast chasms of difference that divide us from other nations and from other cultures. The pleasure of poetry reveals much about the very nature of archetypal realities and the existence of Collective Unconsciousness; otherwise the babble of languages occasioned by the biblical Tower of Babel would surely keep all of us irredeemably divided. Sardello adds that it is only in this imaginal realm of poetry that distinctions are acceptable "to insert themselves so forcefully as polarities."

Isn't this a call to welcome the half-light of not thinking that we have all the answers? Instead of opinionated insistence, following Lao Tzu, whose name actually represents *senex-et-puer*—in other words, "Lao," or old, and "Tzu," both master and child—can we, shouldn't we be more accepting of difference and try living within the tensions of the insistent polarities? Today, total poles of opposition are fractured apart. We could try to imagine a mid-zone, holding the tensions, accommodating the tensions, in a more centered manner. In the lower three worlds—physical, emotional, and mental—the probability of conflict always exists. It is only at the heart level that it becomes possible to transcend basic dualities, to live above duality. And this is the level that poetry aims to express.

Gail Thomas, Ph.D., serves as President and CEO of The Trinity Trust Foundation in Dallas to remake the Trinity River Corridor. She was co-founder in 1980 of the Dallas Institute of Humanities and Culture and served as its Director for seventeen years. Dr. Thomas' life work has been the study and transformation of cities. For over thirty years she has conducted seminars and conferences on cities and city life. She began in 1982 a series of conferences called *What Makes a City?* attended by city planners, artists, scientists, poets, teachers, business, and civic leaders. She was instrumental in the creation of Pegasus Plaza in downtown Dallas and co-chaired the Dallas Millennium Project to restore Dallas' icon, Pegasus, the Flying Red Horse. For the Trinity project, her efforts helped inspire the philanthropic gifts for the design of Dallas' two Santiago Calatrava bridges. She is currently seeking funds to build the Trinity Spine Trail from the Audubon Center in southern Dallas to White Rock Lake. Her book *Healing Pandora: The Restoration of Hope and Abundance* was released in 2009. Her other books include: *Stirrings of Culture*, with Robert Sardello; *Images of the Untouched*, with Joanne Stroud; *Imagining Dallas*; and *Pegasus, the Spirit of Cities*. She has a book in progress entitled *Recapturing the Soul of the City.*

GAIL THOMAS

Entertaining Ideas on Senex & Puer

THE FORMAT OF this year's event—to speak rather than read our papers—is an appropriate way to honor James Hillman. We are "entertaining ideas"—always one of Hillman's favorite pastimes. It is such a puer thing. We are neither establishing laws, nor determining ordinances. No goals and objectives. Not even an outline. We are playfully, joyously entertaining ideas. All of you who have worked side by side with James Hillman know how he loved it.

And so it is fitting that we, each one, enter into his work, James Hillman's, and imagine it forward into the world.

I have tried to imagine myself walking down one of the narrow roads in Thompson, Connecticut, with him, as I have done in the past, entertaining the idea of senex and puer.

This is our conversation:

GAIL: James, first of all, why do you always start with senex? Your book title is *Senex & Puer*. Shouldn't it be the other way around? Why not start with puer? The child grows into the opinionated adult. And in *Senex & Puer*, the *Uniform Edition*, you titled chapter three, "Notes on Opportunism." Why not "Notes on Opportunity?" Leave it open-ended . . . puer-like? Opportunism seems so structured, like all *ism* words.

JAMES: Ah Gail, you have never liked structure, or endings. No closure. As I said in the beginning of that chapter, "'Chance' and 'system' are other words for puer and senex" (2005, p. 96). The more we can understand about senex, about the system, and the way it works, the more we experience the way puer, the opportunity or chance, works in the world. You see, from a system point of view, puer is so random, so open ended. So chancey. Puer existence is based on opportunities. We begin to see an archetypal aspect of existence reflected through this style.

GAIL: Ok. An archetypal aspect of existence. Let's explore that. Let's take the word 'opportunity.' You say it stems from *porta*—entrance, door. So it is an opening. Then you pull this zinger connecting this "opening" to Poros, father of Eros. Now that blows my mind. Openings, pores in the body, veins flowing, ducts, conveying life-delivering essence, but also opening to all aspects of life—doorways . . . to . . . the 10,000 things.

JAMES: Whoa, that's too fast. You're soaring again, like Pegasus. Come back down.

GAIL: Yes, but remember in the Pegasus myth, "Where the hoof hits the ground, a well springs forth and the Muses come to dance and sing." Pegasus in flight gets chancey. I remember what happened to Bellerophon. He thought himself fit company for the gods, and thought he could ride Pegasus to Mount Olympus, but fell to his death instead.

So, James, it does seem so chancey to assume the puer way. And yet, the senex seems to convey a hardening of the arteries, instead of life giving, flowing Eros. Where is the hinge that holds the two together? Is Kairos the hinge?

You speak of *kairos* as the main Greek word for opportunity. You say Kairos is not just an opening; it is the aiming toward the opening. Here are your words: "an opening in the web of fate . . . an eternal moment when the pattern is drawn tighter or broken through" (p. 97).

JAMES: Kairos is always puer. It passes through opportunity into the established order of senex. Kairos is vulnerable to the senex who says, "Prove it. How do you know?" (p. 98).

GAIL: Sounds like my husband. Law demands the "prove it" stance.

James: Yes, and this is what wounds the puer: the "prove it" thing. But puer must always "leave its door ajar, nothing closed down" (p. 98). And this helps us see where the puer wounds come from. Puer wounds are necessary. They allow spirit to come in. And we see this in the puer in gaps of memory, scheduling glitches. "Puer integrity would mean never covering those holes" (p. 98).

GAIL: So senex covers the holes, and shuts puer down. I see this maneuver crop up in my work in the city, specifically in the shadow quality of our city Dallas' affinity for opportunity. Dallas thrives on opportunity. Perhaps all cities do, being centers of commerce and exchange. For me living in Dallas, the puer image would be Pegasus. Springing from the Medusa after Perseus takes on the bold act of cutting off the head of the Medusa. Out springs winged Pegasus, sporting golden wings, the golden wings of opportunity. Heroic, healing the sick, and rescuing the damsel in distress. Doing battle with the monster—the Chimera.

JAMES: Yes, winged Pegasus, like winged puer, like winged Hermes, crossing boundaries, always getting into trouble—trouble for those who try to mount Pegasus to soar to the heavens, like puer Bellerophon, thinking himself fit for the gods, and falling back to earth and to death.

GAIL: Many say Dallas has a new icon. It too soars above the landscape. Santiago

Calatrava, the architect, declares that the Margaret Hunt Hill Bridge has wings, that it is a winged thing, a suspension bridge, suspended across a great divide. Wings over the city. Like Pegasus, puer in flight.

JAMES: Remember that puer consciousness acts as Psychopompos. "Hermetic puer as Psychopompos!" (p. 108). We have had to go to the end of the affliction we are calling 'opportunism' in order to recover the spirit moving in it. Dallas seems destined to be a city of boom and bust. Things seem constantly new here—young, raw, bold, daring. And you continue to draw consequences of brash acts of inflation.

GAIL: True, and yet, this is what you are calling opportunity—*porta*, an open door. But, then, it is not permanent. It cannot be possessed. That door will close. In Dallas, our wound is that we are unable to imagine the door closing. Endings and new life, like senex and puer, seem to be the image of Dallas itself. This was our founding myth—John Neely Bryan coming to Dallas to trade with the Indians and finding the Indians massacred only days before in a raid by Federal troops. So what does he do? He marks off the streets leading to the river, and sends word back to the east coast that there is a new town here—one called Dallas, offering opportunity and new beginnings.

JAMES: Perhaps this is the soul's code for all cities—that there be puer cycles of limitless growth leading ultimately to rigid organization and stagnation. Remember, it is through the wounds in human life that the gods enter. Certainly this is also true for cities.

GAIL: This is important. It is the shadow side of opportunity that stirs soul. Out springs Psychopompos—Guide of Souls—Hermes the Trickster.

JAMES: The soul is awakened in the world through injury and death. It is puer who initiates this action through daring and adventure—through opportunity. Puer as Psychopompos—Guide of Souls.

GAIL: Utilizing what you call the kairotic moment—an opening, a possibility available at a very special moment in time. This is the phenomenon that captures my imagination. This moment. This extraordinary moment when puer reverses into senex, or senex opens to puer. I can imagine this kairotic moment to be when "motion itself" begins, "life itself," when the physical and metaphysical realms desire each other and begin to vibrate. Whoom, out springs Psychopompos!

JAMES: Pure puer, Gail.

And suddenly we realized we had come full circle on this country road in Thompson, Connecticut.

Gustavo Barcellos is a Jungian analyst in São Paulo, Brazil, a member of the Associação Junguiana do Brasil (AJB) and the International Association for Analytical Psychology (IAAP). He is the founding member and Editor-in-Chief of *Cadernos Junguianos*, AJB's annual journal since its inception in 2005. He lived in the USA during the 1980s where he finished his M.A. in Clinical Psychology at the New School for Social Research, and studied at the C. G. Jung Foundation, both in New York City. During this period he met James Hillman, with whom he studied and who was later to become his mentor and friend. After returning to Brazil, he translated several of Hillman's books into Portuguese and is responsible for introducing archetypal psychology to Brazilian students. He is the author of many books and articles in Brazil and abroad in the field of archetypal psychology, imagination and the arts, including a book on the psychology of the brother archetype in 2009, and a book on psyche and image in 2012. He was a contributor to the books: *Listening to Latin America—Exploring Cultural Complexes in Brazil, Chile, Colombia, Mexico, Uruguay and Venezuela* and *Psyche and the City: A Soul's Guide to the Modern Metropolis*, edited by Thomas Singer for Spring Journal Books, to which he contributed the chapter on São Paulo, "Harlequin City." He has been professionally involved with Jungian educational and analytical institutes throughout the country and teaches seminars in Jungian and archetypal psychology. He has held a private practice in São Paulo, Brazil, since 1985.

GUSTAVO BARCELLOS

Notes on Horizontality:
Continuity, Penetration, Soul, the Sibling Archetype

1.

IN AN INTRIGUING chapter of James Hillman's volume *Senex & Puer* (2005), "Notes on Verticality: Creation, Transcendence, Ambition, Erection, Inflation," he clearly sees puer phenomenology and psychology equated with ascending modes of consciousness, with transcendent and vertical directions in soul, with erection and erectability (archetypal and otherwise), and consequently also with ambition, competition, arrogance and what psychology now calls "inflation"—as if puer consciousness ignored "the daily world and its incessant continuity" (p. 159). I want to call attention and concentrate here on this "incessant continuity," in order to create a dialogue with that important essay. Hillman goes on to show us that all those characteristics, if viewed from the puer perspective—and not from our ordinary ego perspective—reveal indeed a truly spirit phenomenology where transcendence becomes a way of transgression, and arrogance, ambition, and inflation could be understood as the emotions working towards "redemption, beauty, love, joy, justice, [and] honor" (p. 175) in the world—aspects we so much lack in contemporary life. But ambition, arrogance, and even inflation take us up. What would take us forward?

To face and struggle with the "incessant continuity" of our daily world, the very idea of a daily world, would lead us away from the puer and closer to soul, moving us from verticality to horizontality: an anti-heroic move. And also an anti-erection move, for we would no longer go for erection per se, or archetypal erection, as with the puer, but for archetypal *penetration*, as with the *anima*, penetration in the horizontal plane—the world (and *not* beyond or away from it).

Erection is not a function of relationship, though magical or even miraculous it may be. "An erection serves less to relate lovers than to ride them heavenward in ecstasy. An arrow, not a bridge" (p. 167). It lacks continuity, being utterly momentary, a moment in time. Maybe continuity is more a predicament of the *anima* than an aspect of the senex. Anima is what gets us involved with something, maintaining us in bonds, penetrating and being penetrated. The verticality of the spirit is intermittent, not incessant. It leaps, has moments of insight, of vision, or the mystic moment. Soul and horizontality seem incessant, for soul is always with us, always there for us, being continuity itself, our continuous and inexplicable complications with the world. What follows ascensionism, verticality, and erection is archetypal penetration into the world.

The "continuity" that does not cease is the world, vale of soul-making. For the world of soul-making is a horizontal world, not ascendant, not transcendent: "Call the world if you please, 'The vale of Soul-making.' Then you will find out the use of the world . . . ," are the famous lines by poet John Keats that James Hillman quotes for his vision of soul work. This is the sphere of relationships and the interpenetration of all things, ideas, people, passions, pathologies, when we are horizontally aligned with the anima as that in us who then penetrates and is penetrated, who senses the world and is sensed by it. From this perspective, to be in the soul, esse in *anima*, is to be in a penetrative mode.

Hillman's work makes it easy for us to see how much we are caught into the conditions of the puer-senex archetype in our culture—conditioned to experience what is new and what is old, what is past and what is old, what is tradition and what is inspiration, every day in our lives and in the world in ascensional terms, with vertical imaginings, ups and downs. Erections and depressions. For if, as Hillman so extensively shows us, verticality is present in the puer, it is as well relevant in the senex. Depression, melancholy, and downwardness are important aspects of senex consciousness. "Saturnine" we call it and feel its leaden weight. Senex consciousness involves us with depth, with the deepening of experiences, with weight, as if always in, so to speak, "downward ascensions." "The way up and the way down are one and the same," said Heraclitus (fragment 60). Or, "the downward and inward pull of gravity into subjectivity," as Hillman has put it (p. 257).

We shall now call upon the sibling archetype and its impact on the world and on our relations to the world and to people, paradigmatic as they are of all horizontal symmetric styles of consciousness. I would like to call attention to this archetype to see how brothers and sisters can teach us the difficult lessons of horizontality, continuity, symmetrical relationships, and soul-making. This means a deepening in the horizontal plane toward the Other, the world, and its events and complications. For it is necessary to imagine and experience depth also in a horizontal plane with a penetrative fantasy. Soul can deepen things also in horizontal connections.

The value of horizontal symmetrical relations for the work of soul-making is stressed by Hillman as early as in *The Myth of Analysis*, his book from 1972, in a long note in Part One, where he states:

> To recreate family in our generation, eros and psyche must have the possibility of meeting in the home; this would favor soul-making. . . . This perspective looks less to the hierarchical connections of parent-child and the issues of early childhood, authority, and rebellion and more to the soul connection, as between brother and sister. . . . [W]here concern for soul is paramount, a relationship takes on more the nature of the brother-sister pair. . . . if soul-making is the aim, then the equality of the brother-sister relation must be paramount . . . (p. 58, n. 56)

Those statements have had a profound impact on me since my first reading of this powerful note back in 1984. What surprised me then most, and still does today, was that such a relevant and strong understanding of a new yet still unnoticed paradigm—not only for psychology but as well for culture—this Aquarian fantasy of horizontality, symmetry, and the importance of nonhierarchical connections was presented in a footnote, that is, in a somehow marginal position, in the borders of reflection, not in the main text. The repression of horizontality was also showing here. I wanted to understand this repression.

2.

The fundamental role of the sibling archetype in structuring and establishing individual adult life is undeniable, yet still dismissed. Brothers and sisters are powerful figures in our lives as we build our mature relationship patterns. Curing the eternal wounds created in these relationships is a lifelong task since these relationships accompany us throughout our lifetimes. However, it is clear that depth psychology and culture in general have neglected to perform a more detailed observation and theoretical reflection on this topic, and instead have focused more intensely on the relationships we build with mothers and fathers. Nevertheless, as a primordial image in the soul, the sibling is present in the psychological evolution of each individual (even the only child) and each culture, and its influence is inevitably projected in history and in the construction of bonds with friends, companions, partners, and colleagues.

I think that psychology must follow the movement that has been detected in other arts and sciences: the current search for the paradigm of symmetry and horizontality. Psychoanalysis, with its three patriarchs—Freud, Adler, and Jung—opened last psychological century with a focus on parental relationships: Oedipus, the hero, and the family. This model has begun to be criticized and revised. The transition to the new millennium could open the twenty-first century with the task of focusing on fraternal relationships.

The experience of the sibling archetype, and the role of the fraternal in our lives, is part of the mythologizing activity of the psyche: even without the literal experience of a blood tie, we search for a sibling and build fraternal stories with friends we so often call "brothers." The field of comparative mythology, folklore, literature, religion, and folk tales has a dazzling array of stories and legends that cast light on the many sides of these ties and their inherent difficulties. There are several sets of siblings and twins in the mythical stories that reach us through various traditions. The wealth of the images is all there and available in myths, fairy tales, stories, and the clinic. Castor and Pollux, Helen and Clytemnestra, Amphion and Zeto, Remus and Romulus, Gilgamesh and Enkidu, Cain and Abel, Jacob and Esau, Hercules and Iphicles, Apollo and Hermes, Apollo and Artemis, Medea and Absyrtus, Exú and Ogun, Isis and Osiris, Cosmas and Damian, the Ibejis, Iphigenia and Electra, Antigone, the sisters of Psyche, the constellation and the sign of Gemini, the third zodiacal house: the territory of siblings. Our topic is very broad. So many patterns, so many faces: from cooperative twinship to rivalry and fratricide. Certainly almost all the founding myths in the Indo-European tradition involve stories of brothers. Each one tells a piece of the larger story of symmetry in human relations. Pairs of brothers appear in many of the stories about founding cities. Amphion and Zeto founded Thebes, Castor and Pollux founded Troy, Remus and Romulus founded Rome, and Cain founded Enoch. Brothers and brotherhood found *polis*, found community.

However, I believe that for psychology and culture the true importance of symmetrical, horizontal relationships can only emerge and make us more aware of their influence when the hierarchical focus on asymmetrical parental relations (which, though loving, will always hide the specter of power and domination) has been abandoned. Only when the lenses of hierarchy have lost their predominant place in our view of the world and of us, and in a linear view of the psyche, can a renewed sensitivity to equality actually step onto the stage. It is all we need. It is the difficult experience of equality, which is at the heart of the sibling archetype, both in our personal lives and on the broader stage of culture and politics.

This "sibling impact," as I call it, translates more precisely into the experience of real assimilation and appreciation of *diversity*. The first and founding experience of diversity, of similarity in difference, which is established when a brother or sister appears (again, either through a blood tie or through a bond of friendship), is important precisely to the extent that it allows us to relativize the monotheistic identification with the model of paternal authority, throwing us into the polytheistic field of horizontal relationships, in the "incessant continuity" of the world, that permits free movement between valid ethical singularities.

3.

In order to understand more deeply the question of sibling love and its importance to soul-making, we should now turn more directly to some aspects of its psychopathology, of its suffering. Here there are two levels that can be glimpsed simultaneously: on the one hand, the wounds that are typical of sibling relations, in the various patterns that comprise a psychopathology of symmetrical relations, and on the other hand, sibling relations themselves as a wound, in other words, the shadow in which these relationships are found in the broader field of history and culture. Being wounded by a sibling, or feeling wounded by a sibling, involves hostility, aggression, and eros. The emotions involved are, therefore, predominantly jealousy, envy, and hatred. But additionally, the sibling is the wound, an area in the soul that is clearly off-limits according to the patriarchy of the Judeo-Christian mythological tradition. Rivalry and envy, jealousy and contention are part of the fraternal constellation because they are deeply rooted in our cultural and religious tradition. The story of Cain and Abel is the paradigm of this wound. Let's take a look at how this particular story speaks to us of this wound.

We recall that Castor and Pollux, for instance, present an older polytheistic tradition of cooperation and fraternal love; Cain and Abel, in our Judeo-Christian monotheistic tradition, represent a pattern of brotherly rivalry and hostility. Castor and Pollux are beneficent: they are healers; they protect men from danger and save sailors. They work together in affinity. Cain and Abel, on the other hand, antagonize each other, compete and disagree, acting separately, as in so many other myths of heroes and gods who are brothers/sisters. The two stories are very different: two aspects of the same bond, two faces of the same love.

According to the story in Genesis 4, right at the beginning of the first book of the Bible and well known to all, Cain and Abel are brothers vying for the attention and love of their father. Their competition turns into a fight that ends in the first murder in Judeo-Christian mythical history. In other words, this history (our history) begins precisely with a murder. What is at stake is their father's favor: Cain, a farmer, offers him the fruits of his labor (fruits and grains), while Abel, the younger son and a shepherd, offers the best of his livestock (a bloody sacrifice of a sheep). This dispute enters into the archetypally larger conflict between an agrarian fantasy and a nomadic fantasy, between farmer and shepherd, between attachment to the land and animal mobility.

The father accepts Abel's gift, thereby indicating the superiority of animal sacrifices over vegetable sacrifices. In a fit of jealous rage, Cain slits his brother Abel's throat with a sharp stone. Cain kills his only brother, and thus kills the possibility of brotherhood, the possibility of symmetry. So Cain becomes the first murderer in history, the inventor of homicide, the revealer of death. Abel, the first man to die, is considered by some to be the first martyr. The God of the Hebrews then decides that Cain can no longer work the land and must instead become an eternal fugitive, doomed to wander east of Eden to the land of exile, the Nod desert, where eventually he builds a city, Enoch. The first child of the first couple receives a severe punishment for his crime.

Especially with regard to the sibling archetype, our mythological and cultural tradition begins with a story of dispute, rivalry, and jealousy between brothers that leads to fratricide and exile. The wound is very deep. Consider this metaphor: exile. From the beginning, the myth places fraternal/sibling relations into an environment of horror, death, and failure. This leads to exile. In a monocentric culture where the Father is the foremost power, there is no place for symmetrical relations. The emotions of envy and jealousy, which are always so corrosive and pathologized, are paradigmatically included in this tale.

Jealousy and envy arise in rivalry, which in turn is the shadow of intimacy and cooperation; it directly harms our capacity to familiarize ourselves, to get familiar with something, and pushes us into "exile." With our siblings we learn to divide and to share, we learn horizontal relations, so our sensitivity to equality starts here. Sibling rivalry, this affront to equality and horizontality, deeply affects our subsequent ability to share, to belong, and to be part of groups and neighborly relations. It therefore affects the amplitude of the soul in the horizontal world. In other words, it affects our experience of community.

But on the other hand, it is through this shadow that we are initiated into the distinctions between friend and enemy, the most advanced and sharp distinctions we should make between companions and adversaries, between familiar and strange, between singularity and otherness. A sibling is both different and same, at the same time, and it is through this paradox that the soul finds its way in the horizontality of the world. Brothers and sisters are the archetypal basis for constructing the Other, and for recreating an idea and a sense of community within the incessant "new orders" of the contemporary West.

4.

Maybe what Jung recognized and understood as *anima* starts as a function of relationship in a horizontal level. If this is so, we can get back now to erection and penetration, where we started—where everything starts—and say that if the *puer* is "up-and-down," *anima* is "in-and-out." In this perpendicular image we all need to perform the puer-psyche marriage, as Hillman also has suggested (pp. 88-89), which for me means asking anybody who acts in the name of soul to find connections "between the puer's drive upward and the soul's clouded, encumbering embrace" (p. 84).

Only when the lenses of hierarchy have lost

their predominant place in our view of the world and of us,

and in a linear view of the psyche,

can a renewed sensitivity to equality

actually step onto the stage. It is all we need.

It is the difficult experience of equality,

which is at the heart of the sibling archetype,

both in our personal lives and on the broader

stage of culture and politics.

— Gustavo Barcellos

Dennis Patrick Slattery, Ph.D., is Core Faculty, Mythological Studies at Pacifica Graduate Institute. He has been teaching for 43 years and is a Fellow at the Dallas Institute of Humanities and Culture. He is the author, co-author, editor or co-editor of 20 volumes, including five volumes of poetry. His recent works are *Day-to-Day Dante: Exploring Personal Myth Through* The Divine Comedy and *Riting Myth, Mythic Writing: Plotting Your Personal Story*. Forthcoming is *Our Daily Breach: Exploring Your Personal Myth Through Herman Melville's* Moby-Dick, a collection of essays on psyche and poetics, *Creases in Culture: Essays Towards a Poetics of Depth*.

Oath-Taking as Scar-Making: Remembering the Original Wound

FEW BOOKS OR essays by James Hillman have revealed the creative workings of his fertile imagination as the chapter "Puer Wounds and Odysseus' Scar" in *Senex & Puer* (2005), volume 3 of the *Uniform Edition*. This essay will track Hillman's understanding of being wounded and its relation to the two psychological figures that may emanate from the wound's suppuration: senex and puer. Odysseus' famous wound, which scar tissue runs through the twenty-four books of the *Odyssey*, comprises the epic figure's signature, his brand, and his being in the world. It is one thing to be wounded, Hillman writes; it is another to survive it. Yet his essay does not get to the epic hero's wounded nature until we have traveled through two thirds of it (p. 235), where Odysseus is shown to be an amalgam of both senex and puer energies and dispositions.

My intention is less to reiterate Hillman's thought on senex and puer but to indicate their relevance to oath-taking in Homer's *Odyssey* (1974). I have identified ten oaths in the epic; the first appears in Book Two, and the last one ends Book Twenty-Four. My intention is to use the figures and forces of senex and puer to imagine more fully oath-making and oath-taking and its importance in contemporary conflicts globally; we may see with a greater understanding the construction of oaths between adversarial parties if the mythic figures of senex-puer were taken into account, adhered to, and imagined into the truce's composition. Together, Homer and Hillman reveal what comprises a sustained agreement between oppositional politics.

To begin, Hillman (2005) insists that "imaginal reality . . . informs puer consciousness" (p. 223) wherein crippling is indispensable for this figure. He achieves a greater viability through his vulnerability. Senex qualities, on the other hand, include "judgment, sobriety, prudence, deviousness, isolation, and suffering," yet he has "little power" (p. 238). Odysseus, Hillman argues, is a combination of senex-puer energies, attitudes, and dispositions. Running parallel with the Greek hero's character and actions is a series of oaths that course like a red thread through the epic, beginning in Book Two and ending in Book Twenty-Four. The oath itself is best grasped as a senex-puer creation that holds energies of both figures in a tension that allows for peace to be constructed and maintained if the terms of the oath are honored by the conflicting energies of seemingly irreconcilable forces. Under the oath rubric I also include pacts, truces, cease-fires as well as other forms of mutually agreed-upon compromises that allow the tension of opposites and oppositions to sustain a harmony through a written code or set of agreed-upon conditions. Here resides one of the contemporary values of Hillman's astonishing insights into the wound. The oath is an extended expression of senex-puer energy that can heal even while it sustains the memory of the original violation, affliction, or wound.

Oaths carry both senex and puer energy and vitality; they also encompass the shadow of the wound that has been inflicted or may be inflicted further in the oath's absence. Following Hillman, an oath has the capacity to parent the wound and the wounded, a quality so necessary today given the increasingly violent instability, decapitations, as well as the increasing numbers of dramatic displacements of citizens fleeing violence and mass murders globally. The puer spirit imagines rather than manages (p. 220). It is the task of the senex spirit to manage. But first the oath or truce must be imagined with great craft and subtlety if it is to "hold" with the necessary stamina to sustain the tension.

Further, an oath can cauterize the bleeding of the puer as he imagines the terms of an oath that is codified by senex consciousness. An oath is a woven marriage between contrary tensions into a fabricated whole even as it contains the scar tissue of the conflict that the oath will both subdue and align. Thus, an oath, which I maintain is a form of myth-making within its deeper crafted design, is crucial for any chance of a lasting peace; nations' leaders must gain some understanding of an oath's mythic dimension, and not simply the political, power-sustaining, or economic implications of these formidable agreements. The mythic dimension is the mucilage in the form of puer and senex consciousness that allows the oath to congeal and hold fast if it is to succeed.

Moreover, an oath or truce is analogous to the scar tissue that knits the wound into a new form. An oath, then, always sustains, as a memory, the haunting reality of the original affliction, its origins and its terms. An oath or truce heals over but does not erase or efface the genesis of the affliction. But the oath as scar tissue is the agent that puts an end to the suppuration or oozing of the original affliction or violation. Along these same lines of development, an oath holds the promise of perduring if it can successfully combine the energies of *metis*, or craft, with *bie*, or force and might. The spirit of the puer is integral to the former, the senex spirit to the latter.

Thus, an oath's success rests on its ability to craft a new reality out of two deeply wounded ones, both of which must sacrifice something of value for the truce to hold. The oath is a witness to this sacrifice. Such a crafting is both mythic and poetic if we consider poiesis as a making, shaping, forming act wherein what was once chaos is molded into a new cosmos. Louise Cowan (1992) has written of epic, "what can be observed from within it activates a full and complete cosmos" (p. 3). Like the formation of an oath, an epic work of the imagination reveals the construction of a new world, even a new order, out of the shards of a dismembered past. Senex-puer energies, held in a carefully crafted tension of opposites, can create the needed restraint essential for the lasting conditions of a new cosmos.

An oath may then act as a gift to both sides of adversity; it has the healing capacity to remove the onus from the wound in order to open both sides to a new, crafted future without bloodshed, theft, or annihilation of the other. According to Hillman (2005), Odysseus himself may be viewed as a mythic figure that resides between senex consciousness—his father Laertes—and puer consciousness—his son Telemachos (p. 241); he participates in both presences. By design and fabrication, Odysseus is a joiner, a maker, a craftsman, and a gushing puer consciousness struggling to keep his mouth shut and to restrain his behavior, initially with limited success as he journeys from Troy to Ithaka. Hillman writes, "In Odysseus the senex urge to persist and endure takes care of the puer spirit that is always ready to risk and die" (p. 239). With an oath, a new reality comes into the world midway between these two contrary forces. His scar is both icon and habitation of such a tension. An oath, like a wound as Hillman describes it, can be "a learner and a teacher both, and has been compared with a mouth" (p. 223). Mouthing an oath with terms agreed upon by oppositional forces can make a new mythos, a new cosmos.

An oath allows a different imagination to intervene (puer energy); it then codifies this imaginal form (senex energy) through an oral or written oath; the connection between puer and senex energy allows for a new way of speaking and stitching the conflict together. In such a practice, an oath stanches the continually flowing blood shed by creating a new vessel to stabilize and thus end the leaking vessel of war's destruction (p. 228). Such an action initiates and places two opposing forces into a third container as a structure that ends the hemorrhaging.

Both senex and puer need one another for an oath to be useful and lasting, for missing in the puer is a psychic container (p. 229); missing in the senex is the imaginative vitality needed for oath construction. Woven into one another, they gain the capacity to create a viable yet always vulnerable code of restraint. The vessel of which an oath is composed may be feminine, a womb of sorts for the senex-puer to gestate within in order to envision further options (p. 229). It buys time for a new birthing and gives space to allow energy to be redirected. The vessel fills in "what is fundamentally missing in the puer structure . . . *the psychic container* for holding in, keeping back, stopping short, the moment of reflection that keeps events within so that they can be realized as psychic facts" (p. 229; emphasis in original). The closed or enwombed nature of the oath as vessel offers a habitation for an open, raw wound to close, or open wounds from both conflicting sides to heal into a new understanding beyond violence as the only effective solution. War—indeed all forms of individual or collective violence—encourages the wound's leaking, seeping, seeking, and suppurating.

The scar of Odysseus is the image his life pivots on: both young puer boy of ten, who is wounded by the hunted boar (XIX, ll. 449-51), and the older senex father, husband, leader, and fighter, whose name and identity curls around the original boar wound: "the scar by which he is known is the mark of soul in the flesh. It is the seal of anima, the somaticized psyche." Hillman continues: as "the scar reminds consciousness of its wobb[ly] uncertainty, the dark vulnerability in the heart of its light" (p. 238), oaths in like manner remind both adversarial parties of *its* and *their* "wobbly uncertainty," which makes the oath both fragile and fierce. What is wise about the wound is contained in its wobbly disposition. In its fragile, wobbly nature, an oath forces both parties out of their treasured and sustaining story. Letting go of the story, Hillman suggests, can then place one within the imaginal realm of image (p. 240). There, image consciousness heals. An oath offers both sides of a conflict an occasion to imagine themselves through the oath's image in a new format of consciousness. The past stories of both sides of an antagonism keeps the wound open; an oath shifts perspective so that both sides can discern that "all parts belong and are co-relatively necessary. . ." (p. 240).

Finally, an oath hopes to construct a pattern of wholeness wherein disparate and conflicting pieces fall into an agreed—right—relation with one another such that they are transformed from pieces to patterned oneness. The union of opposites contains senex-puer consciousness. An oath forms a new image, as a truce, a compact, a binding agreement that grows from arbitration. It allows and encourages a new pattern to emerge, which may happen only after a certain level and intensity of violation and destruction occurs to prompt it.

In Book Twenty-Four, Zeus is the figure of senex energy, whom Athene visits as the families of the slain suitors are donning armor to attack Odysseus and his faithful followers. Athene asks her father, "Tell me when I ask, what plan of yours is concealed here?" (XXIV, l. 474). To which her father replies, first, that she should have thought out for herself how Odysseus would take vengeance on the suitors through war. He then advises, "Since godly Odysseus has done vengeance on the suitors, / Let them solemnize an oath that he may always reign. / And let us bring about oblivion for the murder / Of their sons and kinsmen. Let them love one another / As before, and let there be abundance, wealth and peace" (XXIV, ll. 482-86).

Taking her father's words to heart, Athene approaches the fighting: "Ithacans, hold off from war, which is disastrous, / So you may separate without bloodshed." Then, as the fighting ceases, she addresses Odysseus directly, "Hold off and cease from the strife of impartial war, / Lest Zeus, the broad-seeing son of Cronos, in some way get angry" (XXIV, ll. 542-44). Odysseus, war-weary, but not able to imagine on his own any alternative to end the conflict, "rejoiced in his heart. Then Pallas Athene, daughter of aegis-bearing Zeus, / Established oaths for the future between both sides, / Likening herself to Mentor in form and in voice" (XXIV, ll. 546-48).

Words now have warrior energy in a new form: the oath. The words of an oath structure a new cosmos that rests on trust; trust is the core of the truce and is meant to alleviate the trauma of war. Like a narrative that has been a central piece throughout the journey, an oath is the achievement of, in D. Stephenson Bond's words, "a structured desire" (1993, p. 158) to find and hold energy patterns that complete us in a unique, substantial, and meaningful way. If it can hold in a healthy tension the nature of two competing energies and beliefs, an oath allows both sides to individuate. The oath is then an ongoing wish to remain intact and whole so further development is possible. The oath creates a new living myth from the shards of two previous myths that have been violated, bruised, dismembered, dismantled, and bloody; it then brings them into a form of *sophrosune*, a larger cultural version of the union enjoyed by Odysseus and his beloved Penelope: a balanced harmony. Only on this deeper, mythic, and imaginal level, and not just a practical and political one, can there arise a possibility for reconciliation of both adversaries.

Sarah Jackson is a Jungian analyst, visual artist, and writer. In 2014, she presented a lecture on the female hero in contemporary cinema at the biannual meeting of the New York Association of Analytic Psychology (NYAAP). In spring 2015, she presented "Regarding Images: What Visual Art Can Teach Us About Dreams" to the Northampton Jung Society, in Northampton, Massachusetts, as well as lecturing on the female hero at Simon's Rock of Bard College in Great Barrington, Massachusetts. Jackson is a graduate of the C. G. Jung Institute of New York, and holds masters degrees in Archetypal Psychology and Fine Art. She has taught drawing, color theory, and art history, and has exhibited paintings, drawings, and wall sculptures widely. She lives in Great Barrington, MA, where she has had a private practice for 24 years while raising a daughter. She is now raising a puppy instead, as well as studying tango and dressage.

SARAH JACKSON

Puer Women and Female Heroes

WOMEN WHO OBSERVE and experience the Puer Aeternus, or "eternal youth," as an archetypal element or dominant in themselves may find the existing de-lineations of this archetype—and of the senex, with which it is paired—to be unsatisfactory. Those who have written on the puer with the most nuance and authority—first and foremost Hillman (1979, 2005), as well as Jung (1990b) and Von Franz (1981)—define its essence as quintessentially masculine. Depictions of the hero are similarly restrictive: nearly everything written on the hero up to this point describes that archetype as if it pertained only to men, despite the indisputable existence of female heroes, both mythological and historic. In this essay, I will take a brief look at how the puer and the hero manifest and overlap in women and girls, and how these archetypes are showing up in contemporary culture, particularly in the medium of film.

Those who have written most definitively on the hero—Jung (1990b), Campbell (1949), Kerenyi (1997), and Graves (1960)—and the puer—Jung (1990a, 1990b), Von Franz (1981) and Hillman (1979, 2005)—have concerned themselves almost exclusively with the ways in which those archetypes pertain to men. Even Hillman, who describes archetypal dominants and complexes as transcending gender and having the potential to exist in all of us, writes only about the male puer and the male hero. (When he mentions women and the feminine, his inter-est is in the link between the male puer and hero and the great mother, as well as the mother complex.)

The hero can be understood psychologically as personifying the devel-opment and establishment of the ego; on the mythic level, it relates to the quest for an alliance with the self or psyche. Whether historical or mythological, heroes transcend ordinary limitations; their quests inspire us, as do their struggles to ac-complish tasks, vanquish enemies, and succeed in rescues. The boon or treasure they may or may not manage to obtain, and the knowledge they accrue in the process, benefits others as well as themselves.

The Puer Aeternus, the eternal child or youth, is understood as being synonymous with spirit and opposite to the senex, who is the personification and embodiment of age, time, and limitation. Puer characters and individuals are resistant to both to aging and to being confined by restrictive, repetitive, and mundane tasks and occupations; they remain identified with youth and are frequently fueled by spiritual longing, inspiration, and artistic or intellectual aspirations. A drive toward purification, sublimation, and self-perfection may also be evident, which may also result in narcissistic preoccupation as well as dangerous falls and floundering. Though at risk for accidents and prone to self-destructiveness, the older puer can remain inspiring and vital, especially if both self-acceptance and compassion are cultivated.

As is obvious, none of the above is a gendered description. However, it is equally true that when the puer manifests in men and boys, it does so with a clarity and purity that is part of its nature, and which is unparalleled in other archetypes. Puer men and boys live puer lives and often die puer deaths. Even though this archetype does not present as evidently in women and girls, it most certainly lives in some of us—and of course, the puer refuses to grow up, so we are not likely to grow out of it or it to grow out of us. The Puer Aeternus also shows up in youthful figures of indeterminate gender who refuse to be confined, categorized, or defined in any conventional way as either masculine or feminine.

The puer, as experienced by a girl, can present as an identification with the masculine and a rejection of the feminine—the so-called tomboy—or she may incorporate aspects of both genders, presenting herself more androgynously. A third possibility is an acceptance of her femininity accompanied by a strong pull toward a particular mission, vocation, or calling; such a girl may refuse to identify herself too closely with her mother, or with more normal, and therefore more popular, girls. Regardless of her identification or dis-identification with her gender, a puer girl is likely to find herself inhabiting an alternate reality or separate world. If she tends to be seriously absorbed in some sort of play, this world will be based in imagination and invention; if she is deeply engaged in learning an art or sport, her efforts may well segue into her life's work. Either way, she is likely to feel like the odd one out. Unlike boys with a puer leaning, she may find this a painful predicament.

In puer women, or women and girls with a strong puer streak, the drive to pursue an individual path of both invention and adventure may set her apart, but it may also greatly exacerbate her loneliness. She may feel strongly pulled away and at the same time desire to remain within the fold. The puer girl can be just as inspired, idealistic, and aloof as any boy, but what looks like aloofness may actually be experienced as a kind of self-imposed but unavoidable isolation, and the ensuing loneliness may point toward the senex, as Hillman (2005) has suggested.

Many female heroes have strong puer characteristics, and many female puers are in some way heroic. Female characters with distinctly heroic and puer qualities have been showing up with increasing frequency in contemporary film, which is arguably the medium where our contemporary mythology shows itself most clearly (Jackson, 2013).

These female characters are notable for qualities found in most heroes: courage, perseverance, strength (physical, psychological, and moral), ingenuity, stoicism, and lack of self-pity. However, these women and girls also differ from male heroes in some significant ways. They are often of normal or humble stature and do not rise much in status despite their heroism. Although they are strong and push themselves to their physical limits, they gain more through their intelligence and intuition than through sheer strength. They are often engaged in a valiant but sometimes unsuccessful struggle against evil or malign forces. They seem to be even more frequently betrayed than male heroes, and they are less likely to find help or be rescued by synchronistic occurrences and/or supernatural interventions, so they are often led to make enormous sacrifices, some of which end in death. The vast majority of these women and girls therefore qualify as tragic heroes. Unlike male heroes, whose pride and hubris is often their undoing, these women and girls are more apt to suffer from self-doubt and exhibit a humble attitude. They can, however, be stubborn, willful, and rather proud, especially the historical characters, who can also be quite controlling and strongly opinionated.

These heroic female characters display many puer qualities: they are of course risk-takers and adventurers, and they are also conspicuous both for their youthfulness and their woundedness. (Self-destructiveness is less apparent in these female characters, but it is perhaps no less frequent in actual women and girls.) These characters are indeed driven, in Hillman's words, "to inquire, quest, travel, chase, search, to transgress all limits" (2005, p. 187). However, they usually do so under duress, out of sheer necessity, and for the benefit or welfare of others.

These women and girls also depart from Hillman's characterization of the male puer in two other significant ways. Despite being lonely and sometimes restless wanderers, most of them are not cold, and they neither demonize nor divinize their actual parents. They are, in fact, conspicuous for being either literally or virtually parentless; those with one or both parents still alive have already surpassed them in terms of strength of character and individuation. In this respect, the female characters in these films resemble many of the memorable youthful heroes in modern literature, a great many of whom are orphans. Without parents to protect and support them, they develop their own autonomy, self-reliance, and individuality—qualities that are both heroic and "pueric"—all the more strongly. However, their parentless state accentuates their loneliness and longing. This is particularly apparent in those characters who are motherless.

Of the ten significant female heroes whom I have noted in eleven films[51] over the past decade and a half, seven have mothers who are either dead, crazy, or, in the words of one of those characters (Mattie in *True Grit*), weak and ineffectual. Almost all of the fathers are likewise either dead or missing. Three of the young women are searching for their fathers, one is a child searching for her lost mother, and one is a mother who sends her adult children on a search for their lost half brother. Siblings figure into only three of the films, and consummated romance appears in only two.

The hero who most closely aligns with the male puer, as described by Hillman (2005), is Lizbeth in *The Girl with the Dragon Tattoo* trilogy. She is by far the coldest and most driven among this group of female characters, as well as the most traumatized. She exemplifies one of the characters searching for her lost father; he is a psychopathic criminal who is out to kill her, and she is trying to outwit him in order to save herself. Here the puer is both pitted against yet irrevocably tied to the senex. Like Cronos himself, this father is bent on annihilating his offspring; his child is a fierce young warrior who is equally determined to put an end to him. He is almost completely crippled, both physically and emotionally, utterly bitter, scheming, and treacherous. Even if she succeeds in killing him, Lizbeth may not be able to free herself from him. The negative senex seems to have taken up residence within her and occupies a central place in her trauma complex.

Lizbeth has the most ambiguous gender identity of any of the female characters in this group of films; her Goth presentation—which is also Saturnine, dressed as she is in black, adorned in spikes and chains—overshadows her biological gender. She is apparently a lesbian, but she has sex with a man—just once, and quite impulsively–in a scene that is unforgettable. Mikael, the man in question, with whom she is both friends and partnered professionally, seems much more receptive and emotionally available; she acts as the dominant one and abruptly withdraws after coitus in a way that is at once masculine and also completely congruent with her character. Later on, however, we see her in a somewhat more emotionally intimate relationship with a woman and realize that she is not incapable of tenderness. She embodies the Androgyne, whose essence is imaginal rather than biological (unlike the hermaphrodite) (Rupprecht, 1974).

The majority of the women in these films, almost all of whom are young, are warriors in one way or another. This links them mythically both to the Amazons and to Artemis, as well as to the puer. They exhibit many of the traditional attributes of the warrior hero: courage and strength, of course, as well as perseverance and dignity in defeat. They fully occupy their physicality—instead of their sexuality—in a way that has not been seen before in film. They are pushed, and push themselves, well beyond their physical and emotional limits, driven by necessity and a purpose that is either altruistic, or in some way transcends their own personal concerns and possible gains. Some are wanderers, and most of them experience excruciating uncertainty as well as longing and loneliness, all of which links them to the senex, as described by Hillman (2005, p. 138). They are more susceptible to self-doubt than to inflation, which sets them apart both from the male hero and the male puer, and links them further to the senex.

Hillman describes puer phenomenology as always related to spirit (p. 347). Although some women are certainly driven by a clear spiritual longing, in many others, including the characters in these films, the connection to spirit appears in somewhat more complex, muted, or sublimated forms. The two women in *Crouching Tiger, Hidden Dragon* are dedicated to mastering a martial art that is as much a spiritual practice as it is a form of self-defense. The film's villain, who happens to be female, is also an accomplished martial artist, though of a less disciplined and more nefarious sort. The mission of almost all the female heroes in these films is to reveal the truth so that justice can be done—and both truth and justice are within the realm of spirit (as opposed to soul, which is associated less with truth and more with coexisting narratives and multiple outcomes, amoral as well as moral, unjust as well as fair).

Spirit shows up in sublimated form in the asceticism of anorexics as well as the ritualistic excess of bulimics—and the self-destructive puer is apparent in both. Women's connection to spirit can become complicated and obfuscated by romantic entanglements. This turns out to be especially true when young, heterosexual puer women fall in love with puer or senex men. Such women tend to compare themselves unfavorably to both, which can dash or dampen their own heroic strivings and aspirations. Puer men, especially young artists, musicians, entrepreneurs, and actors, are often too self-centered and relentlessly focused to affirm and appreciate a woman's true genius or gift. Senex men, whether older or younger, can be especially devastating if they are in positions of authority and power—teachers, ministers, and politicians—and especially if they seem to set too high a mark. The lack of real recognition and accurate mirroring—by senex and puer women as well as men—can result in a young woman feeling that she somehow falls short in the ways that really matter to her, even though she is praised for being attractive and, perhaps, smart. Her spirit, which is interwoven with and expressed through the archetypal dominants of both senex and puer, drives her to accomplish, excel, and surpass herself. To the extent to which she cannot, she sees herself as failing.

The heights a female puer tries to scale are her own high standards, and she carries with her a burden that cannot be heroically overcome since she has inherited it from generations of women in her family, as well as her ethnic group, whose ambitions were crushed or extinguished, whose accomplishments remained private and unacknowledged, and whose talents and aptitudes were never recognized or cultivated. When we begin to see truly heroic female characters showing up in novels and films whose load is lighter, and whose fate is less tragic, we will know that further changes are underway, and perhaps then we will also be able to watch the female puer put down her sword and fully unfold her wings.

NOTES

1 For films with female heroes, see Burger, N. (Director). (2014). *Divergent* [Motion picture]. Based on the novel by Veronica Roth. United States: Lionsgate; Coen, J. & Coen, E.(Directors). (2010). *True Grit* [Motion picture]. Based on the novel by Charles Portis. United States: Paramount Pictures; Dery, L. & McCraw, K. (Directors). (2010). *Incendies* [Motion picture]. Based on the novel *Scorched*, by Wadji Mouawad. Canada: El Entertainment; Granik, D. (Director). (2010). *Winter's Bone* [Motion picture]. Based on novel by Daniel Woodrell. United States: Roadside Attractions; Jones, T. L. (Director). *The Homesman* [Motion picture]. Based on the novel by Glendon Swarthout. United States: Roadside Attractions; Lee, A. (Director). (2000). *Crouching Tiger, Hidden Dragon* [Motion picture]. Taiwan: Edko Films; Oplev, N. A. (Director). (2009). *The Girl with the Dragon Tattoo, The Girl Who Played with Fire, The Girl Who Kicked the Hornet's Nest* [Motion pictures]. Based on novels by Stieg Larrson. Sweden: Yellowbird Films; Ross, G. (Director). (2010). *The Hunger Games* [Motion picture]. Based on the novel by Suzanne Collins. United States: Lionsgate Films; Zeitlin, B. (Director). (2012). *Beasts of the Southern Wild* [Motion picture]. United States: Journeyman Pictures.

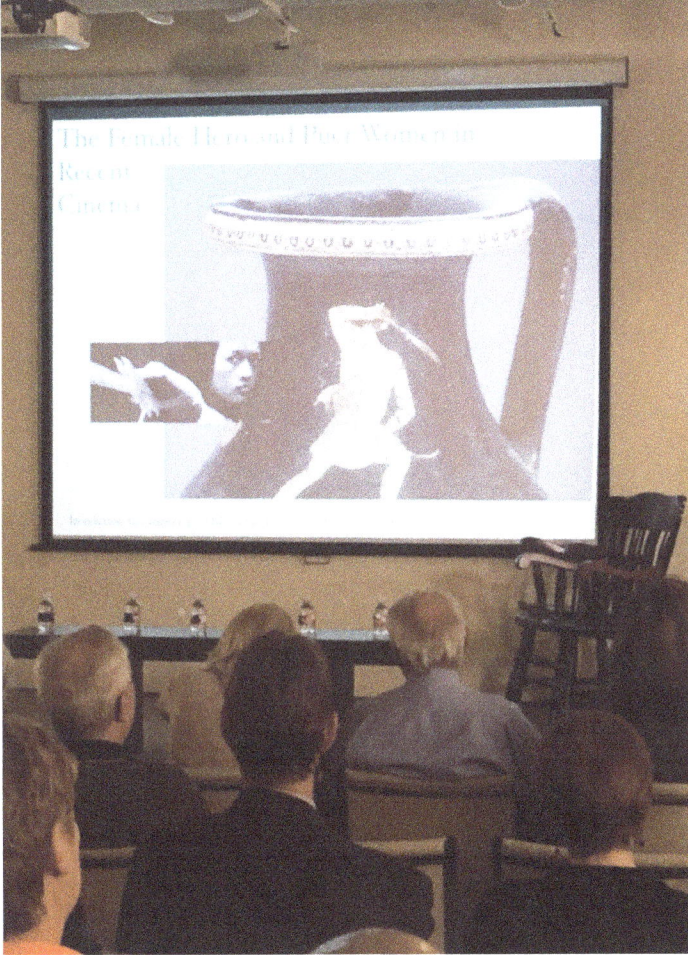

Ill.12 Puer Women and Female Heroes

Matthew Green, Ph.D., is Director of Academic and Social Programs for Cuesta Community College and lead facilitator of the Central Coast Jung Society in San Luis Obispo. For 15 years, he served as an academic director in college study abroad programs, which was the context for investigating the concept and practice of teaching poetic awareness. He presents this experience in a chapter of the book *Reimagining Education: Essays on Reviving the Soul of Learning*, edited by Dennis Slattery and Jennifer Selig, and more fully in his dissertation entitled, *Poetic Awareness: Imagination and Soul in Education*. He has taught and led seminars on depth psychology and culture, and in March 2012, he was one of the speakers at the Hillman Memorial held at Pacifica Graduate Institute.

MATTHEW GREEN

The Senex-Puer Split in The Little Prince

So the soul has come unstrung; its suffering and illness reflect the torn condition of the split [senex-puer] archetype.
—James Hillman, *Senex & Puer*, 2005 p. 40

IN A PASSAGE from chapter one of *Senex & Puer*, James Hillman captures the essence of *The Little Prince* by Antoine de Saint-Exupéry:

> We must further conclude that the negative senex is the senex split from its own puer. He has lost his "child"... Without the enthusiasm and eros of the son, authority loses its idealism. It aspires to nothing but its own perpetuation, leading but to tyranny and cynicism, for meaning cannot be sustained by structure and order alone. (p. 47)

M. L. von Franz, in her classic text *Puer Aeternus*, sees the character of the little prince and virtually every detail of the book as the self-revelation of a man who has fully identified with the archetype of the Puer Aeternus. Other serious folks see the book as a story that celebrates the sickeningly naïve, innocent, and golden hero-child. We might, however, also read this "children's book" as a poetic portrayal of the senex-puer split (and reconciliation): The pilot who narrates the story, in his encounter with the little prince, nostalgically recalls and reconnects with his own puer, his "long-lost child." The little prince, in his adventures, engages and comes to terms (to some extent) with the senex.

The book (1943) opens with the pilot-narrator confessing how, at the age of six, he had to abandon "what might have been a magnificent career as a painter" and adopt the ways and values of the "grown-up" (p. 2). He learned instead to pilot airplanes. What was abandoned was not simply the pursuit of the artist's career, but the very mode that sees with the heart into the invisible qualities and essence of things. ("My drawing was not a picture of a hat. It was a picture of a boa constrictor digesting an elephant . . . Grown-ups never understand anything by themselves . . . " [p. 2]). What was lost was the mode that engages the world with curiosity, enthusiasm and questions, that seeks beauty and connection, that brings inspiration and meaning, and that hears the call to be true to oneself.

The pilot-narrator learned to live among the grown-ups but, like many of us, felt the pang of isolation and alienation from that part of him that could see the elephant inside of a boa constrictor (and a sheep inside of a box, as does the little prince). "And so I lived my life alone," the narrator's confession continues, "without anyone that I could really talk to until I had an accident with my plane in the Desert of the Sahara, six years ago" (p. 3). He then meets the little prince. And the story the little prince tells and the qualities he displays as the two lie stranded in the desert "a thousand miles from any human habitation" (p. 3) is one of the puer exposing and questioning and pushing back against a crusty, arbitrary, impersonal, trivial, and meaningless world in the grip of the senex. The little prince's attention and concern is on apprehending and engaging *l'essentiel* (what is essential) that can only be seen with the heart. The grown-up characters he meets (among them a king, a conceited man, a businessman, and a geographer—"but . . . not an explorer. . . . The geographer is much too important to go loafing about" [p. 45]) instead are preoccupied with "matters of consequence"—authority, acclaim, money, meaningless information.

In the story, it is not just the senex that must learn from and yield to the puer. The book also portrays the evolution of the little prince. He too learns, from the pilot and the fox and his flower, about slowing down and the value of becoming humble, patient, attached, even wounded and nostalgic.

There is not space here to interpret each passage, in the manner of von Franz, and show how the book is indeed a treatise on the senex-puer dynamic. That is something I might suggest that the reader do. Yes, Saint-Exupéry in *The Little Prince* does champion the puer. But doesn't also Hillman. As Glen Slater observes in his poignant Introduction to *Senex & Puer*, "Senex style systems, structures and appeals to authority have tended to dominate our way of seeing, so Hillman enters the problem from the side of puer" (p. xiii).

Saint-Exupéry understands that in literature and art over arguments and concepts puer speaks best for and to puer: "But certainly, for us who understand life, numbers are a matter of indifference. I should have liked to say, 'Once upon a time there was a little prince who lived on a planet that was scarcely any bigger than he was, and who had need of a sheep . . . ' To those who understand life, that would have given a much greater air of truth to my story" (p. 12).

Richard Lewis is a teacher and author and the Founder/Director of The Touchstone Center for Children (www.touchstonecenter.net). Begun in 1969, the Center, located in New York City, is known for its innovative arts and education programs that focus on interdisciplinary explorations of elemental themes of the natural world and the importance of the imaginative and poetic experience in learning. Aside from working with children, he has taught at the Bank Street College of Education, Queens College, Lesley College, Western Washington University, Sarah Lawrence, Rutgers University and CCNY.

His books include: *When Thought is Young: Reflections on Teaching and the Poetry of the Child*; *Living By Wonder: The Imaginative Life of Childhood*; *Taking Flight, Standing Still: Teaching Toward Poetic and Imaginative Understanding* and *I Catch My Moment: Art and Writing by Children on the Life of Play*. In addition to his collection of poems, *Shaking the Grass for Dew*, recent individual poems have been illustrated in *In the Space of the Sky*; *The Bird of Imagining*; *Cave: An Evocation of the Beginnings of Art*; *Each Sky Has Its Words*; *A Tree Lives*; *We Are Rivers*; and *Play, Said the Earth to Air*.

RICHARD LEWIS

A Gathering of Hands

> The puer idea flowers in the air of the moment
> without roots in senex authority.
> — James Hillman, 2005, p. 102

SOMETIMES, WHEN I'M working with young children in a classroom, I ask them to take their hands, and, with their thumbs and second fingers, grasp a piece of the air. And without hesitating, suddenly there are small hands everywhere touching and pinching the breathing of the invisible. No doubts, no questions—just the marvelous momentum and knowing of a child's imagination to understand how to take the world in and through the simple gestures of his or her hands.

In many ways this gift of the child, this sense of play and imagining, is not something a child needs to be taught, but something rooted in yet another profound dimension of childhood: the capacity to wonder. For children, the world, in its very freshness and newness, is a question to be asked, a marvel of happenings and possibility, and, with their instinctual gift for magic and transformation, an unfolding into the hidden of what is the unknown. In many ways this primal 'unknown' is not something simply to be afraid of—but an inviting quality of thought and feeling to be explored and revealed, an unending mystery that lies beneath the very texture of what is alive and awaiting us. And like the young child who came up to me one day and excitedly said, "Oh wow! Air opens, air can open!" it is the child's wondrous seeking and curiosity that allows him or her to suddenly discover how the manifold secrets of the unknown can become, often in an instant, the startling beauty of the known.

Perhaps as adults we are both listener and nurturer to this evolving flowering in childhood, this inborn ability to gather the air between our fingertips—and in a few suspended moments, letting it go. And perhaps, as both participant and imaginer, we too can become, once again, the air itself: breathing, playing, and extending the possibilities of the invisible into something else. Or discover for ourselves, as the Japanese haiku poet Santaro wrote, what we all once knew:

Children are the children of the wind,
The children of heaven,
The children of the earth.

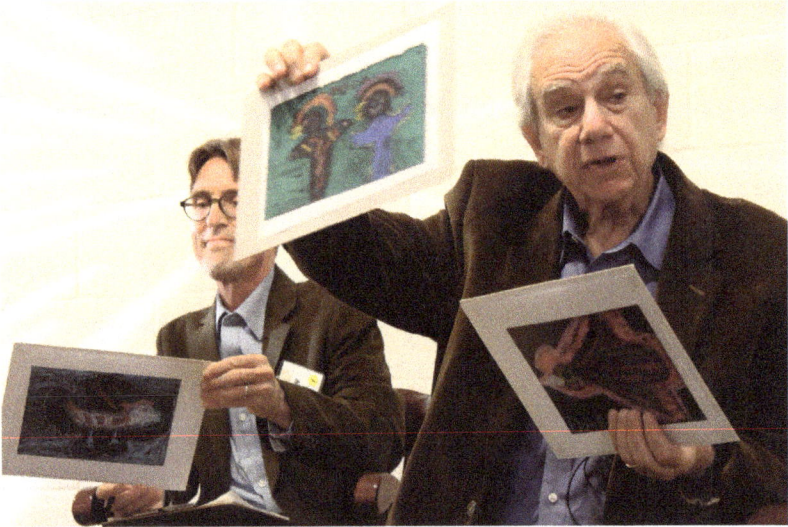

PART IV:

EXTENDING ARENAS
OF SIGNIFICANCE

The Rhythmical Character of Senex-et-Puer
ROBERT SARDELLO

Titanomachy: Finding Senex & Puer in the Twenty-first Century
SCOTT BECKER

The Hidden Senex and the Dying Puer:
A Eulogy to James Hillman's Monotheistic Polytheism
GUSTAVO BECK

Puer Phenomenology: A High Note
RANDOLPH SEVERSON

Robert Sardello, Ph.D, is co-founder and co-director of The School of Spiritual Psychology, which began in 1992, and co-editor of Goldenstone Press. He is author of six books. His main emphasis has been to develop theoretical and practical approaches to perceiving and being in right relation with the Soul of the World, showing that humans are pulled from the time stream from the future rather than pushed from the past, and developing the interior consciousness of the heart. He has created new, yet very practical cultural visions in areas such as the meaning of books, the essence of service, the virtues, money, business, giving, healing, religion, living through the heart, and how to be in right relationship with and in the earth. He is an independent teacher and scholar. He is a Founding Fellow of the Dallas Institute of Humanities and Culture.

ROBERT SARDELLO

The Rhythmical Character of Senex-et-Puer

JAMES HILLMAN'S EXTENSIVE efforts to "see through" what was known in Jung's psychology as two archetypes—that of the senex and of the puer—into his brilliant and scintillating *senex-et-puer* perspective may well be his most important contribution to the creation of Archetypal Psychology.

His efforts accomplish much. Therapeutically, he frees working with the polarities of these archetypes from attempts to awaken the opposite of each other as a kind of balance, into intensifying the qualities of where one is stuck so deeply that surrender ensues. Hillman eventually came to see that what was treated as two archetypal images rather are one. In at least one place, he calls the archetypal image, *senex-et-puer*, the very foundation of psychology, and in another place speaks of the image, when split, as the archetype governing ego awareness.

He provides ways to resolve the polarities of the archetypal image by developing the concept of "sameness," seeing the one within the other—always—thus coming to be able to "play seriously and to "seriously play." He also sees soul as dialogical in character with regard to this archetypal image. Additionally, he points to the archetypal complex of puer-senex tension as coming to resolution in aesthetics, that is, the dimension of knowing through creative, sensory presence. Resolving the two archetypal images into one in the ways that he does, leads, I feel certain, to his concern with the soul of the world, for such resolution is required for full sensory awareness within a "spacious" present.

Two of the archetypal representatives of sameness mentioned by Hillman—Lao Tzu and Christ—take us deeply into the ultimate significance of *senex-et-puer*. The name "Lao Tzu" means: Lao, or 'old,' and Tzu, or 'master' and 'child' alike. Christ many times says, "I and the Father are one." I choose these two representatives named by Hillman to orient us to the fact that his work with *senex-et-puer* enables him to reveal soul as concerned with the deepest past—Lao Tzu-like, as well as equally concerned with the arriving future, Christ-like—simultaneously. This archetypal image carries our deepest concerns, and through his research, Hillman is able to address ultimate questions of life.

Lao Tzu and Christ are two exemplary instances of the varying intensities of soul's enactment deeply in time. The depth dimensions of time do not exactly cohere as sameness, not if the archetypal imagination of *senex-et-puer* is in fact dynamic, changing in intensity, and keeping the past present to the future and the future already present to the past. Archetypal sameness does not quite capture the subtleness of time, wherein successiveness persists together. Let us suggest a complement by looking into the union of persisting successiveness of past and future as rhythm and harmony. This archetype, *senex-et-puer*, I suggest, plays and plays musically.

We are under the archetypal past and future rhythms in many ways. The individual lives within the rhythm of the day, returning to the same/different point every 24 hours. We might say that everyone wakes up as puer and goes to bed as senex. The ego goes through its cycle in a day. We awaken each day with the same/different identity. Our emotional, or soul nature, lives in the rhythm of seven days, and thus the days are named in terms of their archetypal governors—Sunday as "Sun-Day," Monday as "Moon-Day," Saturday as "Saturn-Day," and the rest. Soul rhythm is of a slower rhythm than that of the ego, and we begin to notice, if at all alert, the same/difference of depth-awareness in one week followed by the next one. Our vital life undergoes a rhythm of 28 days before returning to where it was, though now the same/different. The physical body lives the rhythm closer to that of the year. We might say that we start anew as well as age every birthday. If we lived in harmony with these rhythms, it would likely be impossible to become stuck in either the polarity of senex or that of puer.

We are all physically composed of rhythms and harmonies as well, something easy to demonstrate: take deep breath, do not hold it but establish the ongoing continuous rhythm of breathing in and breathing out. While noticing the breath in this way, at the same time, notice the rhythm of your heartbeat. And, while noticing breath and heartbeat, also notice, at the same time, the pulse rhythm. Such a noticing practice can be developed even further—into noticing the biochemical process of the body, such as fluids pouring in and out of an organ, and noticing the intense rhythm of the frontal cortex, a rhythm of 150 million hertz, the exact same rhythm as the sun. We can even become sensitive to the rhythms of molecules, and perhaps even of an atom, where we would notice that the atom is not about speed and multiple particles circling a nucleus like planets, but that the atom is the very origin of rhythm, existing at the boundary of pure stillness and moving substance, a kind of ultimate *senex-et-puer*.

Cosmologies, too, are archetypally governed. We have great difficulty experiencing the persistent successiveness of past and future simultaneity because we are still primarily archetypally governed by the "Big Bang" cosmology. This cosmology governs by splitting.

If everything begins with a gigantic explosion, this explosion has become the template for everything of earth. The theory locating explosion as the beginning continues, now being fulfilled as violence, combustion engines, rockets, war, earth-destruction, conflagration, anger, conflict, natural catastrophes, nuclear melt-down, politics, terrorism, guns, guns, and more guns, cursing, and hatred.

We do not need to know physics to be caught in this unstoppable destructiveness, for the archetype of this kind of physics encompasses us all, and we live within the capture of this cosmology, keeping itself as pure destruction-in-the-making. It is the ultimate senex, in hidden collusion with the split-off archetypal complex of the puer, looking for and promising a future materialism of abundance brought about with ever-new promises of the bright technological future.

The physicist's atom is an artifact of the way of senex investigation. This archetypal vision can only see splitting, and then defending the theory of splitting, by endlessly using the mind to mathematically prove the theory and concoct new ones.

"Scientific" proof of the structure of the atom does not begin in any phenomenological investigation in current physics, but rather by bombarding the atom with light; as they did so, the atom disappeared in the light. So they excited the atom with strong magnetic and electric fields that speeded atoms up, causing an alteration of the atom itself. Atom mean "indivisible." Electrons, protons, neutrons, positrons, and so on, are products of the altered atom. Thus the laws of the atom are unwittingly made to conform to senex physics. We have the dominant of "theoretical physics" rather than a soul physics of rhythms.

The word 'physics' is indeed a beautiful word and means the being-born of the physical world. The cosmos and earth, spoken through the depth of the word "physics," is simultaneously old and new. A physics of the persistence of past and future, at once, a *senex-et-puer* physics does exist. Just a few words about it are warranted here.

Pier Luigi Ighina was an Italian, self-taught physicist. He was born on 23 June 1908, and died in January 2004 at the age of 95, shortly after showing a group of school children some of his inventions. He delighted with the children, saying that they were the only ones who understood him.

Ighina is responsible for numerous inventions, all backed by an archetypal image of physics as *senex-et-puer* in rhythm and harmonies of various sorts. The inventions include a microscope, functioning through fifteen or so microscopes, in tandem resonance, through which it was possible to see the atom, verifying that the atom does not oscillate, but rather vibrates. That is, this physics is one of rhythms and harmonies. He invented a number of demonstrable instruments that use no destructive energy source but are entirely based in the receptivity inherent in varying intensities of rhythms. Among the instruments are an earthquake neutralizer consisting only of strips of multicolored aluminum in the shape of a two cones, one oriented toward the sky and the other toward earth. Evidence exists of its effectiveness. He made another device, also utilizing no destructive energy source, capable of purifying any food matter that comes within its field of action. And he invented a multicolored, moving propeller, also not requiring any destructive energy source for its movement, but slowly rotating above his dwelling in Imola, Italy, that moved clouds into formations for rain or away from each other, revealing the blue, a "simple" matter of understanding resonance. He also discovered that if he changed the rhythmic state of a group of particles, the material itself could transform. On one occasion, Ighina set up his rhythmic apparatus before an apricot tree. After 16 days, by surrounding and immersing the apricot tree in rhythms of a certain frequency, the apricot tree turned into a pear tree.

Ighina discovered what he spoke of as "the Central Atom," or the "Magnetic Atom." He made this discovery with the microscope he made that could magnify one billion times. This central atom of utter stillness brings all other atoms into rhythm and harmony. This discovery is based on his Rhythmic Cosmology[1]–a cosmology that shows how earth creation begins and continues with the forming of Solar Rhythm as inherently in dynamic relation with the forming of a returning, overlapping "depth" Earth Rhythm. The harmony of these two rhythms—the first the rhythmic frequency of golden light, and the second rhythmic frequency, a returning rhythm of sky blue light, brings about the third rhythm, the rhythmic frequency of harmony, or earth, the rhythmic frequency of green light. Earth as a symphony of light. We see earth only as solidity upon which bacteria, insects, plants, animals and humans live, utilizing earth for their own purposes, the human claiming it is all for our own purpose.

We are unable to see the rhythms of creation past containing the future and the future containing the past, both persisting simultaneously because the archetypal complex of a senex-puer split governs us. Living within the spacious presence requires heart-awareness, our middle realm, and earth is also the heart of the cosmos. We were able to surrender to *senex-et-puer* we would see everything as rhythms in symphonic harmony.

NOTES

1 Photographs of the magnetic atom are available on www.rexresearch.com.

We are unable to see the rhythms of creation past

containing the future and the future containing the past,

both persisting simultaneously because the archetypal

complex of a senex-puer split governs us.

— Robert Sardello

Scott Becker, Ph.D., is a clinical psychologist and the Director of the Counseling Center at Michigan State University. Dr. Becker has published in *Spring* and *Death Studies*, and he contributed the psychological commentary to the recent biography, *The Life and Ideas of James Hillman*. He is also the editor of the forthcoming *Inhuman Relations*, Volume 7 of the *Uniform Edition of the Writings of James Hillman*. Dr. Becker's areas of interest are informed by archetypal psychology and include trauma, mourning, dreams, multiculturalism, and astrology. He has also developed an integrative paradigm addressing the negative impact of technology and social media on neurological development and psychological functioning.

SCOTT BECKER

Titanomachy: Finding Senex & Puer
in the Twenty-first Century

HOW DO WE approach such an ancient subject—senex and puer—with fresh eyes? How do we bring eternal images into the present day, and how do we engage them in a way that helps us to envision our future? This is a pressing question since we live in a time when we are increasingly overwhelmed by the digitized, accelerated, and increasingly chaotic world of technological overload, martial violence, and ecological disasters we have unwittingly created and in which we find ourselves immersed. In an attempt to measure the impact of this synthetic, frantic environment on our neurological development and structure, a growing body of evidence demonstrates that our aesthetic and imaginative capacity is eroding, our attention spans are becoming shorter, our capacity to care is declining, and our memories are fading. We are losing our minds, but we don't seem to mind. Said differently, the symptoms of our time are anesthesia, apathy, and amnesia, and together they constitute a powerful threat to our capacity to learn from our past, engage the present, and imagine our future. In short, both senex and puer consciousness are in danger. In this sense, the senex-puer question is in many ways the only serious question, the only one worth asking, but also the most fun: a lead balloon if you will.

Focusing again on the serious aspect of the question, how are we to imagine our danger? What is the myth we are living? These are not easy questions, in a time when our capacity to engage in mythic understanding is itself fading, but if we search our collective memory, our cultural history, we may find an answer. Our guide in this search, as is so often the case, is James Hillman. In his essay (2012), "... And Huge Is Ugly: Zeus and the Titans," Hillman outlined his view that the twentieth century was characterized by Titanism, an inflated, monstrous world created by the absence of the Olympian gods. It is that gargantuan world that our current century has inherited, its gigantism now taking the form of a globalized economy, of digital toys that distract us from the ugliness, of a worldwide web of ever-expanding and ever-more-shallow information, of social media that isolates us from deeper human connection, and of a corporatized global news network that traumatizes us with tragedies broadcast in real-time and in high-definition, even as it obfuscates the truth and distracts us with false comfort. As Hillman pointed out, this inflated world, industrialized, digitized, and globalized, appears in desperate need of an expansive imagination that can check the Titanic excess, an imagination equally vast that provides imaginal vessels, ontological limits, and psychological containers. Hillman suggests that this imagination is fully embodied in the figure of Zeus, son of Cronus, who ends his father's rule and brings back the Olympian gods. We will explore this story as a way to recover senex and puer since Zeus embodies both qualities and offers a way out of Titanic excess and Saturnian oppression.

In Zeus we find an image of the senex as ultimate source of divine law and order: *Zeus Dikêphoros*, harmonizer of the gods and the spirits of the dead; or *Zeus Polius*, guardian of the city. Zeus in this form is the positive senex, the overseer and protector. But Zeus was his father's son. In order to protect his own power, Zeus was willing to swallow the mother of his unborn child, Athena, mistaking her as his future son, fated to overthrow him as ruler of the gods. In this image we find Zeus as the devouring father, the violent bringer of order. So another of his names was *Zeus Kronios*, son of Cronus-Saturn. This image of Zeus places him squarely in the realm of the negative senex, the violent bringer of order, of a Saturnian peace that comes at a price. Cronus-Saturn, we remember, was the ruler of a "Golden Age" in which there was no immorality, suffering, or disorder, but this harmony was achieved only by swallowing his own children. Unity, the myth says, often comes at the price of freedom, of multiplicity. Titanic order, however golden, swallows up Olympian diversity.

But where do we find Zeus today? Jung suggests, in a quote so famous even non-Jungians know it, that Zeus no longer rules Olympus but rather the solar plexus. Jung proposed that we had internalized the gods in our subjective experience and in our symptoms, both personal and political, since they surge forth, as he put it, from the brains of politicians who inflict psychic epidemics upon the world. But this is a modern answer that fails to address the problem at a mythic level. If we return to the story of Cronus-Saturn, who devoured the first five of his children, where is the sixth child? Where is the infant Zeus?

As you may already know, Zeus survived by hiding or, more accurately, by being hidden away. When Saturn came to devour Zeus, Rhea, Zeus's mother, gave Saturn a stone wrapped in swaddling clothes to swallow instead, fooling him and allowing Zeus to grow up in secret, leading eventually to his (Saturn's) castration and overthrow and the release of the other Olympian gods. Zeus forced Saturn to vomit them up, along with the stone he had unwittingly swallowed. The nature of that stone, as well as the manner in which Zeus was hidden, we will reveal later. For now, those details remain hidden.

Before we return to the story, we need to further explore the symptoms we outlined earlier: amnesia, anesthesia, and apathy. In these symptoms we find the impact of the Titanic world. First, we consider the symptom of anesthesia, of what Robert Lifton (1993) called "psychic numbing" and what Robert Sardello (2011) has called "doubling," a state in which we are not fully present to the world, in touch with our own conscience and the animal response of our own bodies. If we consider these ideas in light of recent neuroscience, the implications are disturbing. For example, distinct regions of our brain are losing grey and white matter, in a state of atrophy up to 10 to 20 percent among some high-end, addicted users, resulting in deficits in attention, planning, impulse-control, and emotional perception. Worse, new studies out of South Korea and Germany are showing signs of lateralization of the brain's hemispheres, with the right brain that supports empathy, memory, imagination, and emotional regulation show-ing decreased neural volume and connectivity. In a process described by these researchers as "digital dementia," our brains are becoming lopsided as we focus more and more on processing bits of information and less and less on interacting with each other; more on shallow cognition and less on deeper processes such as integrating and synthesizing information, emoting, engaging others, and imag-ining. If, as the psychologist Harry Hunt has so carefully outlined, synesthesia, the integration of sensory modalities, is the neurological basis of metaphor and imagination, and of consciousness itself, then lateralization and digital dementia have strong negative implications regarding our capacity for synesthesia, which relies in part on the brain's ability to utilize both hemispheres. In Hunt's words, "in terms of the imaginal and numinous we are in dark times" (2015, personal com-munication). In a very concrete, measurable sense, we are losing our depth and our capacity to remember, to care, to focus, and to imagine. The positive forms of senex and puer consciousness are being eroded from within, our peaks and vales flattened by our flat screens. So the first symptom of our time is anesthe-sia, in both the literal and the metaphorical sense: the incapacity to synthesize, to breathe in the beauty and pain of the world, to imagine. Second, we consider the symptom of apathy, found in popular culture in that ultimate expression of adolescent, psychopathic indifference: "Whatever." With a word, anything can be dismissed, along with any trace of thought, reflection, or feeling. We live in the age of "whatever," of apathy on a cosmic scale. "Whatever" negates the world and turns off the mind, ignores the heart, and forgets the soul. "Whatever" is the cry of the negative puer, of freedom from all limits, all obligations, all caring. It is the postmodern form of nihilism—nothing matters, and no one cares. But where does this attitude come from?

One possible answer to this question is the threat of collective trauma. Due in part to the globalization of news media, and in part to the reality of our increasingly chaotic world, we are now exposed to catastrophic incidents, across the street and all over the planet, that have the capacity to overwhelm and shock us, to put us in a state of fight-flight-or-freeze that can lead to a range of posttraumatic stress reactions. We witness, almost in real time, the accidents, the bombings, the shootings, the torture, and the environmental devastation caused by pollution and climate change. We witness all of it, immersed in the flames, suffering with the survivors, adrift in a sea of grief and shock that eas-ily overwhelms our capacity to understand, to feel safe, to reflect and integrate what has happened.

Our minds are capable of disconnecting, running away from the devastation, dissociating our conscious thought from our emotions and our physical bodies. We become numb, disengaged, thinking without reflecting or feeling, not present to ourselves, our pain, or to each other. Our experience is flattened, hollowed out, made two-dimensional and distant. The effect can be dramatic and clinically significant or subtler, but in this state it becomes difficult to remember, to care, to focus, and to imagine.

The shamanic term for this condition is soul-loss: the soul temporarily or permanently leaves the body, and it must be invited back in through a deliberate ritual known as soul-retrieval. The necessity of this ritual on a collective, even global, level has become a real possibility as we all become aware that the world is on fire. We need to shake ourselves awake, invite our animal soul to return so that we can do more than wander about in a dissociative haze. Hence apathy, the incapacity to feel, to engage, to care, should be understood as a symptom of our collective trauma and dissociation. We cannot bear to feel the world's suffering, so we disconnect, float away, click on another hyperlink. Whatever.

Third, we live in a time of amnesia, of forgetting. We are, in both a literal and a figurative sense, losing our personal, cultural, and historical memory. Just one example from neuroscience: in a 2011 experiment published by Betsy Sparrow et al. in *Science Magazine*, college students recalled less information when they knew they could easily access the information later online. Known as the "Google effect," this finding indicates that our brains adapt to the amount of trivial information available via the Internet by preparing to dump the information, not taking the time to encode the information into long-term memory. Neuroimaging of frequent Internet users shows double the activity in short-term memory compared to sporadic users, and this effect becomes stronger each time we use an online search engine. Our brains are becoming symbiotically dependent on our devices. We are, literally, outsourcing our memories onto an external hard-drive. In doing so, we become the negative puer, the flighty, forgetful dilettante, bouncing from Wikipedia to Google to Instagram, allowing the "server" to remember for us, to prioritize the information we consider, to serve it up in palatable doses, and to distract us with something less challenging or less distressing if we become upset or bored or frustrated. The positive senex values of perseverance, a willingness to struggle, to suffer in service of a higher goal, are all being threatened, and the younger generation has no memory of a time when we actually needed to dial the phone, rifle through the card catalog, and search among the stacks of books; actually to read and finish a book for that matter—to focus, concentrate, reflect, and ruminate.

So we need to add amnesia to our list of the symptoms of our time. Perhaps this should concern us, if we remember that memory herself, Mnemosyne, was a Titan who slept with Zeus and gave birth to the nine Muses. Without her, we have no poetry, history, music, dance, tragedy, comedy, or astronomy. In short, without memory, we lose our inspiration and the source of culture. Without the positive senex, we lose the positive puer—the joy that results from a willingness to suffer.

And now we return to our earlier questions: What is the nature of the stone that is offered to Cronus, and where is the child-Zeus hidden? The answers offer a way out of our dilemma.

Zeus's mother, Rhea, fools Cronus by offering him a stone wrapped in swaddling clothes. Most of us know this part of the story, but do we recall the name of the stone? It was called the *omphalos*, the navel-stone, the symbolic center of the world, marked by the point at which two eagles met, one flying from the east and the other from the west. The *omphalos* was sacred throughout the classical world, as it represented the connection between the world of mortals and the gods, the point at which our world is fed by the gods. A version of it rested in Jerusalem, and also at Delphi, where it was the source of the vapors that allowed the oracle to offer prophecies.

After Zeus reached maturity, he challenged his father and forced him to regurgitate Zeus's siblings—Demeter, Hestia, Hera, Hades, and Poseidon— and also the stone itself. In this initial deception, in Rhea's trick, we already find a clue to the difference between Titanic consciousness and the Olympian consciousness that Zeus represents. Cronus took the stone at face value; he failed to see through the ruse, the disguise. Cronus's Titanic perception was literalistic; he lacked the imaginative capacity to perceive that the sacred stone was not literally his son. He swallowed the stone because he failed to understand the symbolic joke, or to see through the symbol as an image, a metaphor. Zeus was, in a sense, the *omphalos*, the world-navel, the divine phallus born of the divine womb, but the symbol is an image, not an icon. Olympian imagination trumps Titanic literalism. This insight suggests that one way of regaining the positive senex is by seeing through the calcified symbols of the negative senex and its absolutism.

And now our final question: after Zeus is saved from Cronus, where is he hidden? Where do we find Zeus the child, Zeus-as-puer? Various answers can be found in different versions of the myth, but the most common story says that he is hidden in a cave on Crete, raised by one or the other of a pair of nymphs, Amaltheia and Adamanthea. Their names mean "tender goddess" and "untameable goddess," suggesting that through our compassion and our wildness we find refuge from the Titanic and regain our Olympian imagination. But there is another version of the story regarding Zeus-in-hiding that further illustrates our earlier point regarding Titanic literalism. In this alternative version of the myth, Zeus is suspended from a tree, neither in the air, nor on the earth, nor in the water since his father ruled all three of these realms. Echoing the earlier deception, Rhea recognizes Cronus's literal attitude: he will search in the air, or on the earth, or in the water, but he lacks the subtle, indirect thinking that would allow him to look somewhere else. Zeus is hidden in-between, in the imaginal realm that in Neoplatonism is called the metaxy. The myth tells us, in the visual image of infant-Zeus suspended from the tree, that Titanism, the negative senex of Cronus, cannot imagine. Titanic consciousness only looks in the air of thought, the earth of the material, physical world, and the water of emotions, not in the space between them. The myth reveals that imagination itself is an antidote to Titanism, and that when we find Zeus we also find the imaginal realm. We discover soul in a cosmic game of hide-and-seek.

In short, without memory, we lose our inspiration

and the source of culture.

Without the positive senex,

we lose the positive puer—

the joy that results from a willingness to suffer.

— Scott Becker

Gustavo Beck is professor of Psychology at Universidad Iberoamericana in Mexico City, where he also graduated, as well as a translator of books and essays on psychology and the humanities, and a clinical psychologist with a private practice in Mexico City. He received a M.A. degree in Mythological Studies from Pacifica Graduate Institute, in Santa Barbara, CA, where he is currently a Ph.D. candidate. His dissertation is an in-depth reading of James Hillman's *Re-Visioning Psychology*. He trained in depth/archetypal psychology at the Instituto de Psicología Profunda en México (Institute for Depth Psychology in Mexico), where he currently teaches and serves as a clinical supervisor. His interests revolve essentially around archetypal theory, particularly regarding its impact over contemporary social, cultural, and political issues. He is a co-founder of and contributor to the *Journal of Archetypal Studies*, which was created in order to foster a broader and more critical conversation around the ideas presented by archetypal theory.

GUSTAVO BECK

The Hidden Senex and the Dying Puer: A Eulogy to James Hillman's Monotheistic Polytheism

> This archetype [the senex] is the one most relevant for the puer.
> By this we mean that the senex is a *complicatio* of the puer,
> infolded into puer structure, so that puer events are complicated
> by a senex background.
>
> —James Hillman (2005), p. 251

LAST YEAR I wrote about James Hillman's work—and about archetypal psychology—as if it were a city, a body politic (Beck, 2015). This year, I want to revisit this city from a different vantage point. Instead of listening to its senatorial debates or paying attention to its democratic struggles, I wish us to see it first from above and, later, from below. To aid our approach, we can start with an image: Let us imagine a raven flying over the city, gazing at the movements of its inhabitants as it glides above its streets, buildings, and monuments. Let us hold that image for a moment, and glide. After some time, let us imagine that the raven tires from its flight and seeks a resting spot, which it finds in the city's graveyard. The raven now stands quietly on a tombstone, carefully observing the hundreds of graves that surround it. After another while, the bird obeys a second instinctual pull downward and jumps onto the ground. It is now standing above a tomb and a corpse. There, standing on the grass, the bird starts to peck the ground under its feet.

This paper is a pecking paper—nothing more and nothing less. It wishes to insert its beak, briefly and bluntly, into some of the corpses of this city's graveyard. Before beginning to peck, however, it might be useful to ask what (or better yet: who) lies under those tombstones? What is the bird pecking? This is starting point for my discussion: Who are the dead in this city? What rotting bodies inhabit this graveyard's underground and what is their role or their importance? Given that this city personifies Hillman's work, to be more precise, we ought to ask whether or not any of the ideas posed by James Hillman in his archetypal psychology have passed away or not. Our working hypothesis is twofold. We will depart from two simultaneous premises: 1) that many of the ideas proposed by Hillman and archetypal psychology are dead, dying, or rotting, and 2) that it is of the utmost importance to archetypal psychology and to Hillman's *opus* that these ideas (and their decomposition) be studied carefully.

To start here, archetypally speaking, implies viewing Hillman's work from the vantage point of the senex. Both the raven and myself are motivated and grounded by this archetypal force. Today, I want to speak about the senex. More important, I want to speak about senex as the archetypal motor behind the process of dying. Even more important, I want to speak about senex as the archetypal motor behind the process of dying in archetypal psychology's ideas.

Or perhaps I should be more radical: I want to speak about the senex as the archetypal motor behind the process of the dying *of and within* archetypal psychology's ideas. For a long time I have had the sense that Hillman's ideas, and archetypal psychology in general, are dying. Also for a long time I have attempted to find palliatives and solutions to this problem. I have tried to mend what I perceive as broken, to stop the process that I smell as decaying, or at least to find some meaning in my mourning. Nothing has worked. This is why today I wish to relinquish my desire for reparation and embrace the movement that I am perceiving: the movement of archetypal psychology towards its own death—the senex drive present in James Hillman's work. Hillman (2005), speaking about "senex emblem of the skull," tells us that it "signifies that every complex can be envisioned from its death aspect" (p. 253). If I follow Hillman, and I follow this movement, speaking about the senex is inevitable. What follows then is that to speak about archetypal psychology's ideas in terms of the senex is to discuss them in terms of their decaying process, of their potential death.

The theme is daunting. There are certainly many reasons not to address the senex. Decay is no easy matter. If we were to imagine, for example, Hillman's *opus* as a corpse, we would need to start asking ourselves some disagreeable questions. Have you ever seen, or smelled, a corpse? It is unpleasant. The vision of a rotting body is not only perceptually traumatic, but also emotionally and mentally difficult to process. Then, there is, of course, the actual process of decomposition. Have you ever witnessed this process in its broader range of stages? It is not only death that is terrifying, but also (and perhaps more so) the movement of death that follows death. Putrefaction starts *pre mortem*: the body starts decaying long before the heart stops beating. All of us, right now, are in fact experiencing putrefaction. I am rotting as I write; you are decomposing as you read. Our bodies are decaying. Can you notice that movement?

Then there is the moment when the senex manifests its presence with most force: when a person becomes a corpse—when someone stops being a someone and becomes a something that is not who he or she was—when a person moves out of his or her personhood and enters the stage of a carcass that has exhaled for the last time and has lost the shine in its eyes. And then it goes on: disintegration *postmortem*. Even after death, the body continues decomposing, slowly becoming unrecognizable and progressively losing its previous form. This is still the senex. According to Hillman,

> [p]utrefaction belongs to Saturn as God of agriculture, dung and dying. Putrefaction in alchemy was natural disintegration necessary for change. Such putrefaction is ferment, decomposition into elements through the release of "sulfuric" aggressive fumes which assault and insult one's sensibilities. (p. 263)

It is this decaying and disintegrative process that I want to engage in now, so I excuse myself in advance for any sulphuric assault and for the possibility of insulted sensibilities. I want to imagine Hillman's body of thought as a rotting corpse, as a decomposing carcass. What would emerge if we stuck to the image of a dying archetypal psychology? What would this type of disintegration reveal? What would this corpse—or the dung in Hillman's ideas—be fermenting or fertilizing? I want to address the possibility that Hillman's ideas are dying, and in that in such dying they are becoming unrecognizable. They are not what they once were. But furthermore, I wish to propose the possibility that this putrefaction, like the death brought by the senex, comes from within. I want to find the senex within Hillman's ideas. Rather than thinking that archetypal psychology is being killed by something external, my hypothesis is that, now that these ideas are four or five decades old, the senex in them is emerging with more strength. Different ideas, of course, may be in different stages of decomposition. Perhaps some of them still have a beating heart. This, however, does not liberate them from the *gravitas* of the senex—from the senex graveness, from the senex grave. When I say that Hillman's ideas are dying, I do not imply that there is something wrong with them; rather, I am suggesting that they are aging and growing old, thus coming closer to their death. The problem would come if we continued reading Hillman's ideas, as many tend to do, exclusively in the terms of the puer. What I wish to avoid at all costs, at least today, is to attempt to heal Hillman's ideas, or try to alleviate their aging process; I would rather us imagine ourselves moving, with the ideas, toward their death. This would imply reading Hillman through the heavy and pessimistic lens of the senex, rather than through the stimulating and always curious eye of the puer.

Hillman's ideas are often depicted as revitalizing and engaging. Those who think favorably about his work frequently argue that it brought life back into the dry and rigidified Jungian milieu of his time. This goes hand in hand with the close association that Hillman's writings hold with the puer archetype. His texts can easily be described as energizing and exciting—even when they are corrosive or hypercritical, they bring with them a sense of promise and possibility. Hillman's style, no one can deny it, has spark. Glen Slater (2005) opens his introduction to the *Senex & Puer* volume of Hillman's *Uniform Edition* with a very Hillmanian sentence: "James Hillman undoes" (p. ix), he tells us. How puer, the usual Hillmanian reader may think: to undo. Shortly, Slater emphasizes it even more: "The undoing," he says, "always becomes an opening." This leap is important because when we speak of "undoing," we still stand in either realm: the puer or the senex—or better yet, we could be located in the tension between the two. Puer undoes; senex undoes—the puer-senex dynamic undoing penetrates even deeper. Undoing as an opening, however, is much closer to the puer. The senex's undoing comes more through collapse and suffocation. The senex undoes us by limiting us and crippling us. Through senex we rot—we are undone from within, through the weight of our own body and its limitations. Now, although Hillman's body of work is clearly embedded in the tension between senex and puer (i.e., it makes a conscious effort to include both archetypal constellations, and explicitly states that one can not be studied without invoking the other), it is also true that Hillman, as Slater states, "enters the problem from the side of the puer" (p. xiii); he "brings puer promise to psychology caught in senex stasis" (p. xvi).

I want, in the few paragraphs that remain, to reverse this. I want to remain within the senex-puer tension in archetypal psychology, but to enter the problem from the other side, the side of the senex. I want to examine some of the inner limitations of Hillman's ideas. I want to find their crippled aspects, their rigidities, and their calcifications. I want also to find the fermenting dung. I want to see if there is any aspect of Hillman's books that is full of shit. For this I have selected a specific idea that is very relevant to the senex-puer theme: psychological polytheism. Allow me to perform an exercise and imagine this notion as an old, rotting, dying idea. Let us say that the particular grave above which our raven is pecking is the one that serves as a resting place for the corpse of Hillman's idea of psychological polytheism.

In 1971 James Hillman published a paper titled "Psychology: Monotheistic or Polytheistic?" There, he argued in favor of a "psychological polytheism" that could allow us to "suspend monotheism, both in our theological judgments and our psychological convictions about stages, about unity, and about [...] advancement" (p. 197). Hillman's argument was a direct attack against the Jungian notion of Self, which he openly associates with Christianity and with the senex. "This archetype might also help account," he says, "for theological monotheism's obdurate persistence, religious intolerance, and conviction of superiority" (2004, p. 196).

Hillman's questioning of the unifying and all-encompassing Jungian Self was not only valuable, in many ways it constituted a revolution in Jungian thought. Hillman really struggled with Jungian orthodoxy and its fixed, monotheistic meanings, which he associated with the senex. It is very likely, in fact, that this is one of the reasons why he preferred to tackle the issue from the side of the puer, in order to stay an ally of multiplicity and polytheism. He tells us: "The job of psychology is to keep senex always in some sort of psychological context, to keep Saturn from becoming paranoid, antisocial, which is potential in his nature. That's why I struggle so with monotheism: I see Saturn in it, his dangerous 'singleness of vision'" (2005, p. 324).

What Hillman fails to notice, however, is that his own approach to senex is paranoid and actually quite monolithic, particularly in that he often neglects the nuances and complexities of the senex. He adopts, in other words, a senex attitude toward the senex. Hillman is so afraid of the singleness of vision latent in the senex, monotheism and Christianity, that he unwittingly falls into the hands of Saturn—he is eaten by its own (originally puer) idea. Of course, since Saturn works (digests) slowly, and Hillman had, in the 1970s, still plenty of puer spark, it took time for these problems to become more evident. Now, however, with age and distance and time, we might see how a senex eye can challenge the once-exciting idea of a polytheistic psychology.

My implication here is that, as the puer halo decomposes and the ideas start to rot, their actual structure is revealed—much like the skeleton is revealed when our flesh recedes after our dying—and leaves us with a very curious possibility: James Hillman writings are not only the playful fiction of a polytheistic, dynamic puer; they are also (structurally) the rigid principles of a monotheistic, authoritarian senex.

This can be seen in many aspects of his approach to polytheism, but allow me to exemplify with two apparent intrusions of the senex in Hillman's ideas about this matter.

The first structural appearance of the senex in Hillman's approach to polytheism is in the argument itself. The mere fact that Hillman titles his essay "Psychology: Monotheistic *or* Polytheistic," (my emphasis) sets the ground for a senex-based discussion of the matter. Hillman (2005), from the start, sees monotheism and polytheism in oppositional terms. As far as he is concerned, these two cannot live simultaneously in psychological discourse. "When opposites appear as a *problem*, so does senex consciousness," says Hillman (p. 271; emphasis in original). Hillman, by posing the issue in the way he does, is planting the seed of the senex. Here we can see a second peck of the senex: the raven not only reveals the structure underneath the skin, but also the contradictions and oppositions present within such structure. The eye of the senex, when examining the corpses of Hillman's ideas, can allow us to see both the structuring contradictions and the contradicting structure that keeps our work moving.

The senex then appears in another inner struggle present in Hillman's idea: in the cultural and historical contradiction implicit in Hillman's model for polytheism. For Hillman, there is one appropriate avenue for being polytheistic: Greece. Hillman does not just want psychological polytheism: he wants a Greek psychological polytheism. He acknowledges that there are "other fantasies," but dismisses them: "These alternatives are less authentic. They are simplistic; they neglect our history and the claims of its images upon us; and they urge escaping from the plight rather than deepening it by providing it with cultural background and differentiated structure" (1975, p. 28). So Hillman basically tells us: to be psychological is to be multiple, *but multiplicity is to be pursued in this one specific way.* This is senex speaking. This is Hillman contradicting himself in the structure of his own argument. This is archetypal psychology struggling with itself. It is also quite curious that Hillman supports his argument with history and structure, two very senex-like traits.

We must remember here that this paper is the story of a pecking raven. My words here are merely poking a corpse, scratching its surface. I am trying to hint at the possibility of Hillman's psychological polytheism rotting. Hillman's idea is certainly deeper and more complex (and thus deserving of much more than pecking) but in order to begin entering the unfathomable Saturnian depths of the senex, we could start by simply contemplating the possibility: perhaps this is an old idea of James Hillman undoing itself from within. It is not my argument that cripples the idea, it is the very structure (how senex) of the idea: a self-contradicting structure which Hillman himself planted in there, and that now, after plowing through the shit, the dirt, and perhaps the corpses, we can begin to harvest.

Perhaps now that I have worked a bit more through the vision of the senex, my initial despair at the prospect of the death of archetypal psychology can be deepened into melancholic reflection. This is another tool provided by the senex: depression as a door into the inner intricacies of phenomena. Maybe the issue is not so much that Hillman's ideas are dying, or that archetypal psychology itself is meeting its end. These are the fears of a young puer. Today, half a century after Hillman's ideas were first posed, it might be important to consider another possibility. Even if the puer aspect of Hillman's work is not dead or absent, perhaps it is simply not as important as it used to be. Maybe the exciting, stimulating energy of Hillman's originality now requires of us, Hillman readers, to perform the tedious, obsessive, repetitive work of the senex. It is time to pay Time its due. In archetypal psychology, the puer is rotting, decomposing, fermenting. The puer in Hillman's ideas is now in a state of permanent putrefaction, feeding the senex, establishing structure, providing ground. Let us mourn the young puer, but also let us allow for aging. Let us welcome oldness. With age, after all, comes wisdom. Hillman's puerile seeds from the 1960s are finally starting to ripen. It is now the season of harvest. It is very likely, I believe, that if we endure the painful path of the Senex, we will find that Hillman and archetypal psychology still have plenty more things to say.

Randolph Severson, Ph.D., is a family therapist and writer whose books include: *Spiritual Existential Counseling; A Catholic Soul Psychology; Adoption: Philosophy and Experience; The Soul of Family Preservation;* and *Adoption: Charms and Rituals for Healing.* Nominated by Congressman Joe Barton, he received the Congressional Angel of Adoption. He was also a Recipient of the Baran-Pannor Award for Excellence in Adoption.

RANDOLPH SEVERSON

Puer Phenomenology: A High Note

Carla came to believe that much more in what the music was about and what it could do. No matter the particular kind of tricky plan you were using, you had to bow down in your feelings whenever the right question was asked with enough oomph to bring back the hot memory of what it felt like to hear someone really take off into the sky of jazz imagination. . . .

—Stanley Crouch (2004), *Don't the Moon Look Lonesome*, p. 11

DR. DENNIS SLATTERY, a poet, critic, and psychologist of note made, at the 2014 James Hillman Symposium, a startling claim: He said he believed James Hillman to be one of the great poets of the twentieth century. Aha. Just so. Just right. That's exactly what he was. Despite reading Hillman for forty years, I'd never seen it with so much clarity. But that's surely the decisive claim, the best description. Hillman had Ezra Pound's scope, Charles Olson's reach, William Carlos William's freshness, the incantatory rhythms at times of *The Wasteland* and of *Howl*; now and then you catch a glimpse of Denise Levertov's glittering stream of limpidity, of Robert Duncan's rosy-fingered Mediterranean radiance, and with his turn to the world, there's Thomas Wolfe and Jack Kerouac—Wolfe on New York City, Kerouac on Denver.

Hillman, a poet? Was Homer a poet? Is the Bible a poem? I would say that Homer was the greatest poet, the Bible, the greatest poem. Bardic, beautiful, encyclopedic, a panoramic embrace of all that is human. That Hillman was a great poet seems to follow. Sing, muse, of the wonder of the soul.

Hillman is more than ideas. Thomas Moore and others have done an extraordinary job disseminating and building on Hillman's ideas. Already, there have been studies of these ideas and more will follow. But Hillman is more than just a set of ideas, and so is archetypal psychology. He was, he is, we are a pulse, a breath, a beat, and a rhythm in movement and speech, a tap-dancing old man, not a few good men, but a few good lines in the poem that is America.

One of the great poets of the twentieth century . . .

Hillman was a great poet because Hillman was a jazz poet. I don't know if Hillman got Jazz, but Jazz got him. Think of his prose, think of his writing. Albert Murray or Stanley Crouch would be his best interpreter. I'm neither one of these, but I do love jazz. Hillman's writing—if that's what we are going to call it—is almost pure jazz in style: it is extraordinarily, frustratingly complex; it's marked by intricate, strong propulsive rhythms; it's improvisational, characterized by those extraordinary riffs, virtuosic solos; it's free, wide-ranging and yet there's always something essentially Hillman about it, some essential melodic line. As Joanne Stroud (2014) said in introducing her paper last year, and indicating why she would not bother to distinguish formally between her words and Hillman's: "When it is exactly right and seems perfect, it's Hillman; when it's not, it's me." The dazzling variations in harmonic structures can make one Hillman paragraph, one book seem to clash with another, but it's Dave Brubeck at Pacific or maybe Hillman at Pacifica, the discord adding to, extending the emotional range of the whole, not detracting from it. If you've ever edited Hillman, you know that the text often looks like a musical score: additions, deletions, arrows, insertions, underscores, blocks, and circles. It was like he was writing for five different voices, five different musicians. As Gustavo Beck (2015) put it, "Hillman's pages are constantly speaking among themselves, arguing, pushing, yielding, dissenting, persuading and . . . betraying each other. It is this textual democracy that keeps Hillman's writing imaginally alive" (p. 60). Yes, textual democracy is jazz. Hillman's texts do converse with one another. Jazz is conversation—"a nuanced, swift and complicated one" as Wynton Marsalis says (qtd. in Koch, 2013).

Music is spirit. Language is soul. Music that is language, that is conversation, is jazz, spirit finding soul, the union of puer and psyche. Language that is musical, language that is jazz: melodious, metered, democratic, conversational is soul-finding spirit, psyche-finding puer. And like jazz at its best and at its worst, Hillman perseverates; he goes on and on. Hillman is always saying the same thing, but he never says it the same way twice, and if it's not said the same way, it's not the same thing. The cover is the song, the standard—the song, the standard made new. Stardust covered thousands of times, each one different from the rest.

And to the portal that is jazz, to the nature of jazz as an aesthetic medium and order, there are few better guides than Hillman (2005) on *pothos* or Hillman (1981) on the color "Blue," which first appeared in the poetry journal *Sulfur* alongside poems by Pound and a review of Olson. Hillman was a great poet because he was a jazz poet. Everything good in America comes out of the Delta. Régis Debray, the great revolutionary and revolutionary thinker said in his book *DeGaulle: Futurist of a Nation* that the twenty-first century will be governed by nationalisms of culture or nationalisms of the tribe. Every thing good in America comes out of the Delta because American culture as it burst into life, into music in the twentieth century, is jazz. Jazz is the American idiom, as Albert Murray said, "the embodiment of the American experience, the American spirit, the American ideal" (qtd. in Holley, 2013). It's Fitzgerald—he had no armor, it was said of him—Fitzgerald's Jazz Age; it is a young man with a horn; it's Biederbecke and Armstrong; it's Miles and Chet.

It's the beat poet. The beat poets weren't just influenced; they imitated jazz—the spontaneity, the improvisation, the "first thought, best thought" philosophy, the repetition of a phrase, the breath as a basic unit. Ginsberg (2001) said of Kerouac: "Yeah. Kerouac learned his line from—directly from Charlie Parker, and Gillespie, and Monk. He was listening in '43 to Symphony Sid and listening to 'Night in Tunisia' and all the Bird-flight-noted things which he then adapted to prose line" (p. 146). It's Martin Luther King, whose sermon style was certainly jazz inspired. "The sermon might have folk roots," writes Garry Wills (1995),

> but it was an art form in continual process of refinement, its practitioners skilled critics of each other, improvers of the common store of themes and tropes. Improvisation as a tradition made the great sermonizers resemble jazz artists or blues interpreters. The sermon verges always on music. . . . The sermon, like jazz, is capable of the utmost sophistication in what it can incorporate. . . . Only in sermon form did religious thought inspire King. He did his school exercises, as a jazz musician might perform his scales at a classical musical conservatory; but he came alive only when the classical devices were put in a jazz idiom. (p. 216)

It's Jack Cole and Bob Fosse in dance; it's JFK, the eternal young President, at a press conference, young man not with a horn, but with a podium, feint, jab, grin, riff in a stylish, velvety musical interplay of call and response conversation. American street life, urban life has always been jazz: the energy, the vibe, the diversity, the freedom, the constant experimentation and thrust beyond the limits, the extremes. It's white and black, and black and white, but most of all it's blue, a blue note comes out of the blues interacting with classical, its energy and elegance, the rawness of the street and the refined restraint of the symphony hall.

Young man with a horn. Jazz is so puer. So puer. It's Gabriel. It's stardust. It's when the saints go marching in. Think Bix Beiderbecke—do you know his story? He and Louis Armstrong were the first two great jazz soloists, but where Armstrong played hot, emotional, an engaged virtuoso showman, Beiderbecke was intellectual. He played pure and cool, aloof from the audience, staring at his feet, emphasizing melody, a style influenced by classical music and French Impressionism; the sound, it was said, like a woman saying yes. Like Joyce's Molly Bloom, perhaps, "Yes, yes, I will, yes" (1986, p. 644).

Born in Iowa, in 1903, Beiderbecke's grandfather was a Mississippi riverboat Captain. A prodigy, he began playing the piano at two, and, between school expulsions and arrests and other mysterious and seedy behavior, he learned his craft on riverboats and in South Side Chicago speakeasies. He hit the big time quick with the Paul Whiteman Orchestra, the self-styled "King of Jazz." But the pitiless touring and the compulsions of the bottle destroyed him. On his last recording he played on Hoagy Carmichael's classic original *Georgia on My Mind*. He died in a hot Queens hotel room, where he'd been living, thrilling or incensing his neighbors with his late night piano playing, at age 28; trembling, screaming, hallucinating about two Mexicans under the bed who were trying to kill him, falling into the arms of his rental agent who, hearing the commotion, had run to his room. A female physician called to the scene pronounced him dead.

Beautiful and damned. The Jesus and James Dean of jazz. Inspiration for the movie *Young Man with a Horn*. Aloof, doomed, alcoholic, blind to shadow, self taught, opportunistic, restless, a drifter, mysterious, vulnerable, shady, pure, amoral, sweet, celestial, a victim, unable to ever get a foothold in life, unable to come to grips with it—"I fall upon the thorns of life, I bleed" (Shelley, 1820, p. 331)— crashing spectacularly, dying young, Beiderbecke was the archetypal puer taking wing on a high note. In his music Gabriel hovered. Row, row, row your boat, blow, blow, blow your horn, life is but a dream.

Bix Beiderbecke. Jazz. America. The puer. Archetypal psychology as a puer psychology. It is in this essential identification of puer with archetypal psychology, and of American jazz as the essential puer archetypal style, that the future of archetypal psychology resides. It's that jazz note in Hillman's work that I sometimes miss in those of us who are trying to do him justice. To do him justice, you know, is to respond first to his aesthesis, the beauty of his prose, his poetry. The style is the thought, the medium the message. To breathe it in and breathe it out, to gasp with wonder, and to respond, as well as we can, in kind. A jazz band, cool cats, beat poets, Pentecostal preachers. Not Eranos but the A Train and Azusa Street. In pursuit, then, its reversion, its epistrophe, the method of archetypal psychology. It's back to Beiderbecke and Armstrong, to the Count and the Duke, to Fitzgerald and his indescribably beautiful prose, to Kerouac to whom beat meant beatific, to the rhapsodic sermons of Martin Luther King, the grace and wit and subtle interplay of a Kennedy press conference. Everything good begins in the Delta. It's back to the South, back to that indelible mix and confusion of cultures that made every jazzman heir to both Bach and the blues. (Read Stanley Crouch on Coltrane. Read Stanley Crouch on everything.) It's back to the South that archetypal psychology must go, which it has, in a manner, with the journal *Spring* migrating downriver to New Orleans, to the birthplace of jazz and the city to which Faulkner went to learn to write, and then maybe, like some of the early blues and jazz men, on to Dallas and Deep Ellum, on to the edge of Freedman's Town in Dallas where this Institute sits and where Hillman lived when he made his famous turn to the world. Back to a style of discourse, unpredictable, free flowing, deviant, disarming, improvisational, sensual, rhythmical. To the blue note of an inexhaustible imagination. It's that blue note, that jazz note that is defining, defining of Hillman's style, defining of our culture, defining of what is best about archetypal psychology and that which makes it so distinctively American. Remember Bly? Remember that great poet's description of Hillman that can clash, like a Brubeck flourish, so discordantly on a Freudian or

Jungian ear: "The most lively and original psychologist we have had in America since William James" (qtd. in *Kinds of Power*, 1997, back cover). An American psychology. Archetypal psychology as an American psychology. More William James. More stream of consciousness. More jazz. More all that jazz, than Viennese or Swiss. What's under works up and what's under archetypal psychology is an angel, is the American Khidir, is Gabriel with his horn. Rod Serling knew it: one of the best and most famous of the early *Twilight Zone* episodes, his version of Capra's iconic *It's a Wonderful Life*, starred Jack Klugman as a suicidal, washed-out trumpet player saved by a mysterious ghostly jazz man, who in a final scene when asked for his name says: "Call me Gabe."

Hillman's life was an American Life, and his style and psychology, an American style and psychology; American Adam, Huck and Jim on a raft, City Lights in North Beach; it's a James Dean, Montgomery Clift, Bix Beiderbecke, Route 66, *On the Road*, puer psychology. John F. Kennedy was born 29 May 1917, Thelonius Monk, 10 October 1917, Dizzy Gillespie, 21 October 1917, Charlie Parker, 29 August 1920, Dave Brubeck, 6 December 1920, Kerouac, 12 March 1922; Hillman on 12 April 1926. Miles Davis, 26 May 1926, Ginsberg; 3 June 1926; Bob Fosse, 23 June 1927, Martin Luther King, 15 January 1929; Chet Baker, 23 December 1929, James Dean, 8 February 1931. F. Scott Fitzgerald's *The Jazz Age* was published in 1922. Bix Beiderbecke died 6 August 1931. The Jazz Age was the jazz decade—the roaring 20s, a breeding ground for genius, for breath, for the breath of genius, spirit, *pneuma*, wind, "not I but the wind that blows through me" (Lawrence, 1971, p. 250), wind instrument, the trumpet, the sax, puer. Where does that leave us, we archetypal psychologists of the twenty-first century, we to whom Hillman has passed, perhaps, not a torch but a trumpet? As Louis Armstrong is said to have voiced about the definition of jazz, "If you have to ask, you ain't never gonna know."

James Hillman tap dance video

Margot McLean

REFERENCES

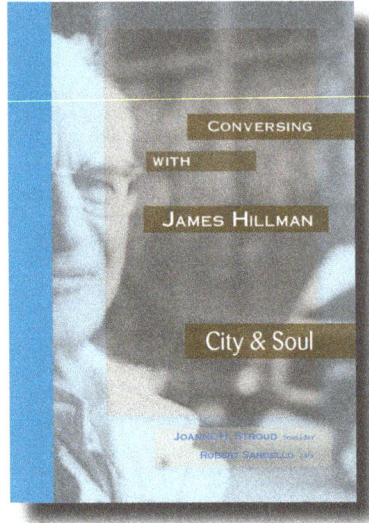

Conversing with James Hillman: City & Soul

Joanne H. Stroud, Series Editor & Robert Sardello, Volume Editor
ISBN-13: 978-0-911005-56-1, Paperback 178 pages, color images

From the 2015 James Hillman Symposium on

City & Soul, Uniform Edition Vol. 2 by JAMES HILLMAN

"Never has James Hillman's wisdom concerning the splitting of the archetype Senex/Puer been more pertinent. Here at the Dallas Institute's annual 2015 Hillman Symposium and in this volume Conversing we bring forward twenty-first century creative thoughts and suggested possibilities for understanding why old and new are charged with such dissension." —Joanne H. Stroud

Conversing with James Hillman: Senex & Puer includes works by: James Hillman, Gustavo Barcellos, Gustavo Beck, Scott Becker, Tom Cheetham, Matthew Green, Nor Hall, Sarah Jackson, Cheryl Sanders-Sardello, Robert Sardello, Randolph Severson, Dennis Slattery, Joanne H. Stroud, Rodney Teague, and Gail Thomas.

Established in 2014, the *Conversing with James Hillman* series publishes the papers from the James Hillman Symposia, held annually at the Dallas Institute of Humanities and Culture. Each symposium takes as its subject a volume of the *Uniform Edition of the Writings of James Hillman*. Internationally recognized scholars write papers that explicate the volume and illuminate concepts developed by James Hillman in his ground-breaking work on archetypal psychology. The title of the series, *Conversing with James Hillman*, emphasizes the dialogic nature of this work, considering Hillman's texts in psychological, philosophical, historical, cultural, and social frameworks. Edited by series editor, Joanne Stroud, and volume editor, Robert Sardello, *Conversing with James Hillman* supports the mission of the James Hillman Symposia to honor Hillman's lifelong study of—in his own words, a "psychology deliberately affiliated with the arts, culture, and the history of ideas, arising as they do from the imagination."

References

Beck, G. (2015). "Returning to the soul's body politic: Reflections toward an imaginal democracy." In J. Stroud & R. Sardello (Eds.), *Conversing with James Hillman: City & Soul* (vol. 1). Dallas: Dallas Institute Publications.

Berry, J. (2001). "Democracy and all that jazz." *Los Angeles Times*. Retrieved from http://articles.latimes.com/2001/jan/21/opinion/op-14966.

Bly, R. (1988). *A little book on the human shadow*. New York: HarperOne.

Bond, D. S. (1993). *Living myth: Personal meaning as a way of life*. Boston: Shambhala.

Burns, K. & Ward, G. (2000). *Jazz: A history of America's music*. New York: Knopf Doubleday.

Butterick, G. F. (1980). *A guide to the maximus poems*. Berkeley: University of California Press.

Campbell, J. (1949). *The hero with a thousand faces*. New York: Pantheon Books.

Cheetham, T. (2015). *Imaginal love: The meanings of imagination in Henry Corbin and James Hillman*. Thompson, CT: Spring Publications.

Corbin, H. (1988). *Avicenna and the visionary recital*. (W. Trask, Trans.). Princeton: Princeton University Press.

Corbin, H. (1995). "Mundus imaginalis, or the imaginary and the imaginal." (L. Fox, Trans.). In *Swedenborg and esoteric islam* (pp. 1-34). West Chester, PA : Swedenborg Foundation.

Corbin, H. (2003). "From Heidegger to Suhrawardi: An interview with Phillipe Nemo." (K. Raine, Trans.) *Temenos Academy Review*, 6.

Cowan, L. (1992). "Epic as cosmopoesis." In L. Cowan & L. Allums (Eds.), *The Epic Cosmos* (pp. 1-26). Dallas: Dallas Institute Publications.

Crouch, S. (2004). *Don't the moon look lonesome*. New York: Vintage.

Crouch, S. (2006). *Considering genius: writings on jazz*. New York: Basic Civitas Books.

Debray, R. (1994). *Charles de Gaulle: Futurist of a nation*. (J. Howe, Trans.). New York: Verso.

Dickinson, E. (1864; 1998). "#802; The spry arms of the wind." In R.W. Franklin (Ed.), *The poems of Emily Dickinson* (Variorum ed., p. 757). Cambridge: the Belknap Press of Harvard University.

Donahue, J. (2014, April). Interview with Jon Curley. *The Conversant*. Retrieved from http://theconversant.org/?p=4453.

Duncan, R. (1996). *"Opening the dreamway."* In J. Hillman (Ed.), *Opening the dreamway: in the psyche of Robert Duncan. Spring: An annual of archetypal psychology and Jungian thought*, 59. Woodstock, CT: Spring Publications.

Gilligan, C. (1982). *In a different voice*. Cambridge: Harvard University Press.

Gilligan, C., Lyons, N. & Hammer, T. (Eds.). (1982). *Making connections: The relational worlds of adolescent girls at Emma Ward School*. Cambridge: Harvard University Press.

Ginsberg, A. (2001). *Spontaneous mind: Selected interviews*, 1958-1996. New York: Harper.

Graves, R. (1960). *Greek gods and heroes*. New York: Doubleday.

Hillman, J. (1960). *Emotion*. Evanston, IL: Northwestern University Press.

Hillman, J. (1967). *Insearch: Psychology and religion*. Putnam, CT: Spring Publications.

Hillman, J. (1972). *The myth of analysis: Three essays in archetypal psychology.* Evanston, IL: Northwestern University Press.

Hillman, J. (1975). *Re-visioning psychology*. New York: Harper & Row.

Hillman, J. (1979). "Senex and puer." In Hillman, J. (Ed.), *Puer papers* (pp. 3-53). Dallas: Spring Publications.

Hillman, J. (1981). "Alchemical blue and the unio mentalis." Sulfur, 1 (1), 33-50.

Hillman, J. (1981). *The thought of the heart and the soul of the world*. Dallas: Spring Publications.

Hillman, J. (1996). *The soul's code: In search of character and calling*. New York: Random House.

Hillman, J. (1995). *Kinds of power: A guide to its intelligent uses*. New York: Doubleday.

Hillman, J. (1997). *Archetypal psychology: A brief account*. Woodstock, CT: Spring Publications.

Hillman, J. (2004). *Archetypal psychology* (Uniform ed., vol. 1). Putnam, CT: Spring Publications.

Hillman, J. (1971; 2004). "Psychology: monotheistic or polytheistic?" In Archetypal Psychology (Uniform ed., vol. 1). Putnam, CT: Spring Publications.

Hillman, J. (2005). *Senex & puer* (Uniform ed., vol. 3). (G. Slater, Ed.). Putnam, CT: Spring Publications.

Hillman, J. (2006). *City & soul* (Uniform ed., vol. 2). (R. Leaver, Ed.). Putnam, CT: Spring Publications.

Hillman, J. (2007). " . . . And Huge Is Ugly: Zeus and the Titans." In Stroud, J. (Ed.), *Mythic Figures* (Uniform ed., vol. 6). Thompson, CT: Spring Publications.

Hillman, J. (2007). *Pan and the nightmare*. Putnam, CT: Spring Publications.

Hillman, J. (2010). *Alchemical psychology* (Uniform ed., vol. 5). Putnam, CT: Spring Publications.

Homer. (1974). *The odyssey*. (A. Cook, Trans.). New York: W. W. Norton.

Holley, E. (2013, August 24). "What Albert Murray taught us about jazz." *A blog supreme from NPR jazz*. Retrieved from http://www.npr.org/sections/ablogsupreme /2013/08/24/214831904/what-albert-murray-taught-us-about-jazz.

Hoyle, F. (1965). *Of men and galaxies*. London: Heinemann.

Hunt, H. (2015). Personal communication.

Jackson, S. (2013). *The female hero and the animus* (Unpublished master's thesis). C. G. Jung Institute of New York.

Joyce, J. (1986). *Ulysses* (Vintage ed.). (H. Gabler, Ed.). New York: Random House.

Jung, C. G. (1960a). *The structure and dynamics of the psyche*. In G. Adler et al. & R.C.F. Hull (Eds. & Trans.), *Collected works of C. G. Jung* (Vol. 8). London: Routledge & Kegan Paul.

Jung, C. G. (1960b). *Mysterium conunctionis: An inquiry into the separation and synthesis of psychic opposites in alchemy*. In R.C.F. Hull (Trans.), *Collected works of C. G. Jung* (Vol. 14). London: Routledge & Kegan Paul.

Jung, C. G. (1984). *Civilization in transition*. In G. Adler & R.C.F. Hull (Eds. & Trans.), *Collected works of C. G. Jung* (Vol. 10). Princeton: Bollingen Series, Princeton University Press.

Jung, C. G. (1990a). *Symbols of transformation*. In R.F.C. Hull (Ed. & Trans.), *Collected works of C. G. Jung* (Vol. 5). Princeton: Bollingen Series, Princeton University Press.

Jung, C. G. (1990b). *The archetypes of the collective unconscious*. In R.F.C. Hull (Ed. & Trans.), *Collected works of C. G. Jung* (Vol. 9i). Princeton: Bollingen Series, Princeton University Press. Original work published 1934-1950.

Kelly, R., Quasha, G., & Stein, C. (1974). "Ta'wil or how to read: A five-way interactive view of Robert Kelly." *VORT* #5, 2 (2), 108-34.

Kerenyi, C. (1997). *Prometheus: Archetypal image of human existence*. Princeton: Princeton University Press.

Koch, Katie. (2003, 13 April). "Jazz as conversation." *Harvard Gazette*. Retrieved from http://news.harvard.edu/gazette/story/2013/04/jazz-as-conversation/.

Lawrence, D. H. (1971). "Song of a man who has come through." In V. de sola Pinto & F. Warren Roberts (Eds.), *The complete poems*. New York: Penguin.

Lifton, R. (1993). *The protean self: human resilience in an age of fragmentation*. Chicago: University of Chicago Press.

Merleau-Ponty, M. (1945; 2003). *Phenomenology of perception*. (C. Smith, Trans.). London: Routledge.

Moore, T. (1994). *Soul mates: Honoring the mysteries of love and relationship*. New York: HarperPerennial.

Packer, M.J. (1985, October). "Hermeneutic Inquiry in the study of human conduct." *American Psychology*, 10 (40), 1081-1092.

Quasha, G. (forthcoming). "Uncertainties." In P. Joris & P. Cockelbergh (Eds.), *A city full of voices: Essays on Robert Kelly*. New York: Contra Mundum.

de Rougemont, D. (1981). "Hérétiques des toutes les religions . . . ." In C. Jambet (Ed.), *Henry Corbin. Cahier de l'Herne*, 39. Paris: Consacré à Henry Corbin.

Rupprecht, C. (1974). "The martial maid and the challenge of androgyny." *Spring: An annual of archetypal psychology and Jungian thought* (pp. 269-93). New York: Spring Publications.

Saint-Exupéry, A. de (1943). *The little prince*. (K. Woods, Trans.). New York: Harcourt Brace Jovanovich, Inc.

Sardello, R. (2011). *Acts of the heart: Culture building, soul-researching; introductions, forewords, and prefaces*. Great Barrington, MA: Lindisfarne Books.

Serling, R. (1960). "Passage for a trumpet." In Don Medford (Dir.), *The Twilight Zone*. Culver City, CA: Metro-Goldwyn-Mayer Studio.

Shelley, P. B. (1820; 1977). "Ode to the west wind." In W. H. Auden & N. H. Pearson (Eds.), *Romantic Poets: Blake to Poe*. New York: Penguin.

Slater, G. (2000). "Archetypal fundamentalism in the twenty-first century." In D. Slattery & L. Corbett (Eds.), *Psychology at the threshold*. Carpinteria, CA: Pacifica Graduate Institute Publications.

Slater, G. (Ed.) (2005). Introduction. *Senex & Puer* (Uniform ed., vol. 3). Putnam, CT: Spring Publications.

Sparrow, B., Liu, J., & Wegner, D. (2011, 5 August). "Google effects on memory: Cognitive consequences of having information at our fingertips." *Science Magazine*, 333 (6043), 776-778. doi: 10.1126/science.1207745.

Stroud, J. (2014, October). "Return of the soul to the world." Paper presented at the James Hillman Symposium, Dallas Institute of Humanities and Culture, Dallas.

Tacey, D. (1998). "Twisting and turning with James Hillman: From anima to world soul, from academia to pop." In A. Casement (Ed.), *Post-Jungians today: Key papers in contemporary analytical psychology*. New York: Routledge.

Varnedoe, K. (2006). *Pictures of nothing: Abstract art since Pollock*. Princeton: Princeton University Press.

Von Franz, M-L. (1981). Puer aeternus: *A psychological study of the adult struggle with the paradise of childhood*. Sigo Press.

Wallenda, N. (2014). *Balance: A story of faith, family, and life on the line*. New York: Hachette.

Wills, G. (1995). *Certain trumpets: The nature of leadership*. New York: Touchstone.

Yau, J. (2006). "Passionate spectator: On Frank O'Hara's art criticism." In *The passionate spectator: Essays on art and poetry*. Ann Arbor: University of Michigan Press.

James Hillman Symposium 2016
Alchemical Psychology

Inaugurated and supported by friends of James Hillman and by scholars of his founding work in archetypal psychology, the James Hillman Symposium is the leading forum for an ongoing discussion of the *Uniform Edition*, a 11-volume collection of his writings, co-published by the Dallas Institute and Spring Publications. The mission of the conference is to encourage conversations about Hillman's major ideas and concepts in conjunction with psychological and cultural topics as well as pay tribute to his life and career.

Each of the James Hillman Symposiums takes for its subject a volume of the *Uniform Edition of the Writings of James Hillman*. The symposiums encourage participants to deepen their understanding of Hillman's writings by listening to talks given by leading scholars in diverse fields of psychology, art, theater, litera-ture, and film—united by an appreciation of James Hillman's innovations—and by contributing to lively, stimulating discussions.

The October 2016 James Hillman Symposium will address Hillman's fifth volume, *Alchemical Psychology.* With this volume, Hillman intends, in his own words, "to give psychoanalysis another method for imagining its ideas and pro-cedures by showing how alchemy bears directly on psychological life." Hillman becomes our guide as we explore the colors, chemicals, vessels, and fire of alchemy with the co-mingling streams of archetypal psychology's psyche, soul, and myth.

Join us to explore this brilliant work and to celebrate the life and ideas of James Hillman. Once again the conference will take place at the Dallas Institute of Humanities and Culture, located in lively Uptown, Dallas, Texas. *Alchemical Psychology* is available for purchase from the Dallas Institute's online bookstore as well as from Spring Publications.

For more information, please visit www.dallasinstitute.org.

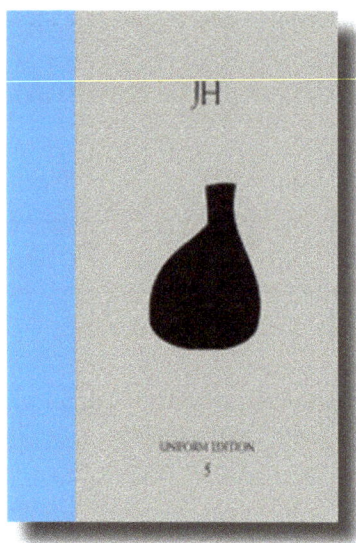

The 2016 James Hillman Symposium on

Alchemical Psychology
Uniform Edition Vol. 5   by JAMES HILLMAN
ISBN-13: 978-0-88214-583-9   first edition, hardcover 350 pages

This book collects all of James Hillman's papers on the alchemical imagination from 1980 to the present: "Therapeutic Value of Alchemical Language"; "Silver and the White Earth I & II"; "Alchemical Blue and the Unio Mentalis"; "Salt: A Chapter in Alchemical Psychology"; "Rudiments: Fire. Ovens, Vessels, Fuel, Glass"; "The Imagination of Air and the Collapse of Alchemy"; "The Yellowing of the Work"; "White Supremacy"; "Concerning the Stone—Alchemical Images of the Goal"; "The Azure Vault: Caelum as Experience."

"Those who have worked hard at their studies of nature, alchemy, and the soul will be richly rewarded with this exquisite volume. At times, it is easy to confuse James Hillman's writing with Jung's work—they both sparkle with uncanny brilliance. But, no one—perhaps not even Jung—can penetrate to the strange realm where psyche and natural substances commingle—the psychoid realm. Hillman brings the substances and their operations to life in the most poetic, tangible way possible. Here's just one phrase among many hundreds that sings out to me: where he is describing the Stone, he alludes to "the loneliness of distance and the insensitivity of style as certitude" (p. 240). The book is a collection of mostly previously published works that is well worth reading a hundred times over, but Hillman devotees will jump for joy with some new material. This book is a tribute to one of the deepest works by this prolific scholar. *Alchemical Psychology* is one of the most authoritative and profound books ever written on the subject." *(review by Thom F. Cavalli)*

UNIFORM EDITION of the Writings of James Hillman

The uniform, clothbound set of 11 volumes of the writings of James Hillman (also available as ebooks) unites major lectures, occasional writings, scholarly essays, clinical papers and interviews—arranged thematically. Each volume is embossed with a drawing by the American artist James Lee Byars.

ARCHETYPAL PSYCHOLOGY
Uniform Edition Vol. 1

CITY & SOUL
Uniform Edition Vol. 2

SENEX & PUER
Uniform Edition Vol. 3

FROM TYPES TO IMAGES
Uniform Edition Vol. 4   (Available in 2017)

ALCHEMICAL PSYCHOLOGY
Uniform Edition Vol. 5

MYTHIC FIGURES
Uniform Edition Vol. 6

INHUMAN RELATIONS
Uniform Edition Vol. 7   (Available Fall 2017)

PHILOSOPHICAL INTIMATIONS
Uniform Edition Vol. 8

ANIMAL PRESENCES
Uniform Edition Vol. 9

CONVERSATIONS AND COLLABORATIONS
Uniform Edition Vol. 10   (Available Fall 2019)

ON DEPRESSION
Uniform Edition Vol. 11   (Available Fall 2018)

Order a book: www.springpublications.com or www.dallasinstitute.org/publications

What Is the Dallas Institute?

For over thirty years, the Dallas Institute has conducted original programs that enrich and strengthen the cultural heart of our great city. Our house on Routh Street is home for those who enjoy reading, thinking, exploring, and discussing timeless ideas that make us most fully human. The Institute has been described by our members as a "sanctuary," as an "oasis," as a "place for reflection," as "food for the soul."

Our members are the lifeblood of the Institute. It is for them that we create classes, groups, programs, and events that bring the wisdom and imagination of the humanities into their lives. If you are already a member, we thank you. If you aren't, please think about becoming a member, and join us on a common journey toward the discovery of truth, beauty, and all else that is good and noble.

The Institute's purpose is to enrich and deepen lives through the wisdom and imagination of the humanities. The humanities, as we treat them, are the written things and the spoken stories that help us define ourselves as human beings—literature, history, philosophy, politics, psychology, and mythology, among other fields.

Since 1980, the Dallas Institute has conducted public programs aimed at discovering what the humanities have to offer to the cultural life of the city, and we accomplish this through classes and group studies; through public and professional seminars; through conferences and civic involvement; through programs for school teachers and principals; and through publications.

Mission

The Dallas Institute of Humanities and Culture is a nonprofit educational organization whose purpose is to enrich and deepen the practical life of the city with the wisdom and imagination of the humanities.

The Dallas Institute accomplishes its purpose through programs for school teachers and principals, general courses of study, public and professional seminars, publications, conferences, and civic involvement.

Vision

The Dallas Institute of Humanities and Culture, a beacon for imaginative thought, dialogue, and programs grounded in the wisdom of the humanities, is helping to shape in positive ways our quality of life today—our conduct, traditions, decision-making, problem-solving, and creativity.

Find out more about the Dallas Institute http://dallasinstitute.org

The Dallas Institute of Humanities and Culture

2719 Routh Street, Dallas ,Texas 75201   214- 871-2440

INDEX

Index

light, 7, 40, 44, 47, 64, 75, 84, 105–6, 110
limitations, 47, 87, 120
loneliness, 88–90

M

makeweights, 15, 37, 42
Marsalis, Wynton, 14, 126
masculine, 12, 87-88, 90
Medea, 76
Medusa, 70
memory, 9, 11, 58, 70, 82, 109, 111–13, 125
Merleau-Ponty, Maurice, 48–49
metamorphosis, 37, 63
metaphor, 40, 77, 111, 113
metaxy, 114
mindless newsertainment, 9, 58
Mnemosyne, 112
mother complex, 87
mundus imaginalis, 51, 55
Muses, 70, 112, 125
mythical, 10-11, 13, 36, 39-40, 66, 80, 87, 109-110
myths, 11, 13, 38, 59, 67, 71, 74-77, 85, 109-10, 113-14

N

narcissism, 9, 58
Neoplatonism, 114
neuroscience, 110, 112

O

Odysseus, 11, 81, 83–85
O'Hara, Frank, 53–54
omphalos, 113
opening, 11, 69–71, 119
opportunity, 10–11, 63, 69–71
opposites, 7, 9–10, 12, 15, 45–46, 59, 63, 66–67, 81–82, 84, 121

www.ingramcontent.com/pod-product-compliance
Lightning Source LLC
Chambersburg PA
CBHW061222270326
41927CB00022B/3472